THE BIRTH OF MONOTHEISM

THE BIRTH OF MONOTHEISM
The Rise and Disappearance of Yahwism

By André Lemaire

Translated by André Lemaire and Jack Meinhardt
Edited by Jack Meinhardt

Managing Editor – Steven Feldman
Designer – Sean Kennedy
Production Manager – Heather Metzger
Editorial Research – Bonnie Mullin

This book has been published with the support
of John P. Merrill, Jr. and Carol Jennings Merrill.

Library of Congress Cataloging-in-Publication Data:

Lemaire, Andre, 1942-

[Naissance du monotheisme. English]

The birth of monotheism : the rise and disappearance of Yahwism / Andre Lemaire.

p. cm.

Includes bibliographical references

ISBN 978-1-880317-99-0

1. Monotheism--History of doctrines. 2. God (Judaism)--History of doctrines. 3. God--Biblical teaching. 4. Bible. O.T.--History of Biblical events. 5. Bible. O.T.--Theology. 6. Middle East--Religion. I. Title.

BL221.L4613 2007

296.3'110901--dc22

2006101696

© 2007
Biblical Archaeology Society
4710 41st Street, NW Washington, DC 20016

CONTENTS

INTRODUCTION

The birth of monotheism? How can that be? For many people, the notion of an all-powerful, universal, creator God is simply the Truth. And the Truth is simply the Truth, always and everywhere. It doesn't get "born."

That may be so, but truths do get discovered, and the discovery of a truth is the birth of an idea. The basic laws of motion operated in the world before Kepler described them and Newton gave them a mathematical formulation. What Kepler and Newton did was to give coherent shape to forces that govern the physical universe; they gave "birth" to laws of nature. The birth of monotheism is something like that, an idea about the nature of the universe that was born during the Israelite captivity in Babylon.

This book is the work of a historian. It does not deal with metaphysical questions regarding the existence or nature of God. The historian asks, How and under what circumstances did the monotheism of the biblical tradition appear in human history? This kind of inquiry may be less ambitious, but it nonetheless strikes at the heart of one of the world's most influential ideas, one that serves as the basis of Judaism, Christianity and Islam.

For the student of ancient history, there are three principal kinds of evidence: contemporaneous epigraphy (inscriptions dating to the period in question), archaeological remains and literary sources. Although ancient inscriptions provide a direct link to the past, they are rare and often survive only in fragments. Archaeological remains from the Land of Israel are abundant, and they tell us a great deal about the material life of the biblical Israelites; unfortunately, however, these material remains provide only minimal help in understanding the beliefs and hopes of the people who left them behind.

The richest source of information about the biblical Israelites is, of course, the Bible. There are a number of problems, however, in using the Bible as a history text. The Bible was not written all at once by trained historians with access to reliable documents. Rather, it was written by a number of people over a long period of time; and large sections of the Bible were rewritten or re-edited at a still later time (often for propagandistic reasons). Consider, for example, the Book of Isaiah, which is so important for the study of monotheism. Although the Book of Isaiah is attributed to the prophet Isaiah, son of Amoz, who lived at the end of the eighth century B.C.E., that is probably and partially true only of Isaiah 1-39; the rest of the book, Isaiah 40-66, or, at least 40-55, was probably written by an anonymous author (called Deutero-Isaiah, or Second Isaiah, by modern scholars) who lived in Exile in Babylonia in the mid-sixth century B.C.E. At some point, these two sources were combined into a single source, the Book of Isaiah.

Much of the Bible reflects this kind of historical complexity, and scholars frequently debate the date and historicity of biblical texts. Inevitably, a history like this one, which relies in large degree on the Bible, will be a "partial" history, and this partial history will have to deal with texts about which there is no unanimity of opinion. When working with disputed texts, and when trying to fill in history for periods for which the sources are few (and often for which the extra-biblical sources are nonexistent), it is necessary to form working hypotheses that can be corrected as new discoveries are made. It is essential, however, that these provisional hypotheses be consistent with all available documentation.

The term "monotheism," belief in only one god, is so familiar to us that we might forget that there are other forms of religious worship.

Since some of these forms of worship are important in a discussion of the birth of monotheism, it will be useful to say something about them. Monotheism, as the belief in a single universal God, is opposed to "polytheism," the belief in several gods. It might seem that these two forms cover the entire spectrum of belief; but a lesser-known form of belief— one very common in the ancient world—is "henotheism," belief in only one god while leaving open the question of the existence of other gods for other peoples. Henotheism often takes the form of a tribal or national religion; the members of a tribe worship only their god, whom they believe is stronger than any other tribe's god.

Monotheism, polytheism and henotheism designate forms of belief, that is, theological or philosophical concepts about the nature of the universe. Another set of terms describes forms of cultic practice. The term "monolatry" refers to worship of only one god without denying the existence of other gods; thus the religious practice of the henotheists is generally monolatrous.*

A final set of terms is used to classify religions according to the name of their principal deity. For Israel, we will speak of "Yahwism," the religion of the God of Israel, whose name is written with four Hebrew consonants, "YHWH," called the tetragrammaton (for a discussion of the pronunciation of this divine name, see the Appendix). Other religions include "Baalism," the religion of the Canaanite-Phoenician deity Baal, as well as "Mazdaism," the religion of the Iranian god Ahuramazda.

The use of the same term, "Yahwism," to refer to a religion that existed for a long period of time does not imply that the religion remained unchanged. As we will see, the "Yahwism" at the turn of the era is very different from the "Yahwism" of Moses' day. Originally monolatrous, Yahwism

---

*Convention often opposes monolatry to "idolatry," which literally means the worship of idols (or images of deities). This opposition is curious, because one might think the term "mono-latry" (worship of one god) would be the opposite of a term like "poly-latry" (worship of several gods)—much as the opposite of "monotheism" is "polytheism." Moreover, the opposite of "idolatry" (worship of images) should be "aniconism" (prohibition of the worship of images). These two facts—the absence of a word like "poly-latry" and the opposition of "monolatry" to "idolatry"—are explained, in part, by the development of religious ideas in the biblical tradition. The forms of polytheism encountered by the Israelites—in Canaan, Egypt and Mesopotamia, for example—were all characterized by divine representations: If polytheistic religions were always idolatrous, there was simply no need for a term like "polylatrous."

changed over time, sometimes gradually under its own momentum, sometimes dramatically under the pressure of authoritative reforms or international politics. Then, during the sixth-century B.C.E. Exile, somewhere in Babylonia, Deutero-Isaiah gave Yahwism a universal expression, and monotheism was born.

There was, however, still a history to be lived: The development of monotheistic Yahwism did not stop with the genius of Deutero-Isaiah. It took a long time for this idea to become dominant in religious thought, and even longer for it to become common in practice. Inevitably, though, the rise of monotheism led to the disappearance of certain monolatrous and nationalist aspects of Yahwism and, later, to the disappearance of the divine name. After giving birth to a universal monotheism, Yahwism itself disappeared for good once the Romans destroyed the Jerusalem Temple of YHWH in 70 C.E.

CHAPTER 1

Before YHWH

W hen we think of Yahwism, we think of the religion practiced by the Israelites after they settled in the Land of Israel under the leadership of Joshua: A coalition of clans united by their worship of Yahweh, their national god, who was served at various regional shrines by a class of priests. In addition, Israelite worship was organized around extended families, the *beit ab* ("house of the father"), who also offered sacrifices to Yahweh at local shrines and household altars.

But Yahwism did not emerge from a vacuum. What do we know about religious worship in the southern Levant (the lands of the southeastern Mediterranean littoral) before the appearance of Yahwism?

Most of our epigraphic information about southern Canaanite cults of the Late Bronze Age (16th century B.C.E. to the early 12th century B.C.E.) comes from the Amarna Letters,[1] some 300 cuneiform tablets found in Middle Egypt at Tell el-Amarna, the capital built by Pharaoh Akhenaten (c. 1359-1342 B.C.E.). The Amarna Letters are diplomatic correspondence of the Egyptian pharaohs Amenhotep III, Amenhotep IV (Akhenaten), Smenkhkere and Tutankhamun; they are written in Akkadian, an East Semitic language attested in both southern Mesopotamia (Babylonia) and northern Mesopotamia (Assyria). This correspondence includes letters exchanged with important rulers, petty kings and other officials throughout the eastern Mediterranean and Near East, including Canaan, which was then an Egyptian protectorate. Among the cuneiform tablets are letters to or from rulers in Hazor, Akko, Megiddo, Taanak, Shechem, Gezer, Jerusalem and Lachish.

Unfortunately, the Amarna Letters give a very incomplete portrait of religious worship at Canaanite sites. The information we have consists primarily of evocations of some divinities and theophoric names, that is, names incorporating the appellation of a deity (the name "Abibaal," for instance, ends with the name of the Canaanite god Baal). These sources mention the West Semitic goddesses Anat, Asherah (Athirat), Astarte and Beltu, and the West Semitic gods Baal, Dagan, Hadad, Milk ("King"), Sidq ("Justice") and, perhaps, Ilu/El. They also mention such Egyptian deities as Amun, Hathor, Seth/Baal and Re-Harakhte, as well as the Hittite god Teshub, the North Syrian goddess Hepat and the Mesopotamian gods Bashtu and Marduk, among others.

The various iconographic representations from Canaan in this period are difficult to interpret, as they generally lack inscriptions. It is often impossible to determine whether a statue or relief carving represents a human being or a god; and even when the figure can be unambiguously identified as divine, we often don't know the god's name.

In the absence of any Canaanite mythological or ritual texts, the evidence of the Amarna Letters suggests only that Canaanite religion was polytheistic, comprising a number of gods and goddesses who may have been represented by images or statues.

This picture is clarified somewhat by some 13th-century B.C.E. mythological and ritual texts excavated at Ugarit, an ancient city located on the Mediterranean coast of modern Syria.[2] Although Ugarit lay north of the land of Canaan, these texts probably reflect, to some degree, the general West Semitic cultural features of the Levant as a whole. The documents reveal a polytheistic religion of about 30 deities with anthropomorphic characteristics. At the head of this pantheon is a divine couple, the El bull ("father of humanity," "creator of the creatures") and the goddess Athirat ("procreatress of gods"). In the myths, the young god Baal (also called Haddu/Hadad) plays a very prominent role. Baal (whose

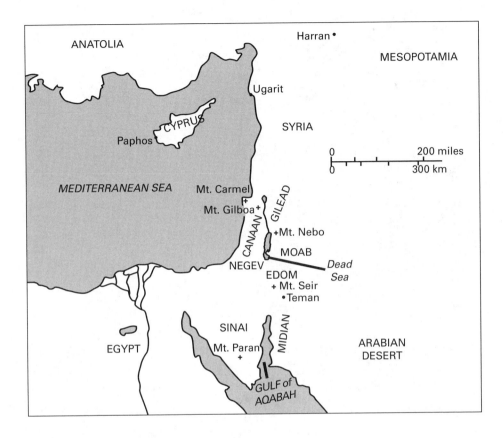

name means "Master") confronts his adversaries, the gods Mot (Death) and Yam (Sea), vies with his rival, Athtar, and consorts with his sister/mistress, Anat. The list of gods in these cuneiform texts also includes Dagan, Astarte, Shapash (Sun), Yarih (Moon) and Rashap.

The numerous ritual texts specify the various sacrifices (animal and vegetable) and other offerings (generally precious metals) made to the various deities. These offerings were probably made at temples devoted to the gods, and several such temples have been excavated at Ugarit.

One Levantine people mentioned in the Amarna Letters is the Habiru. The Habiru apparently lived on the fringes of Canaanite society, inhabiting the central hill country of Israel and possibly serving on occasion as mercenaries of petty Canaanite kings.[3]

Although we do not have any Habiru documents, the Akkadian term 'Apîrû (Habiru) of the second millennium may be cognate with the

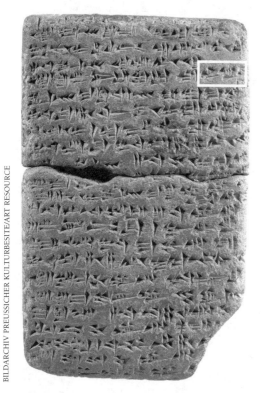

LETTER FROM JERUSALEM. Among the hoard of cuneiform tablets known as the Amarna Letters–correspondence from the Egyptian royal archives of the 14th century B.C.E.—is this tablet, sent by Abdi-Heba, ruler of Jerusalem (written here as "Urusalim" and shown in the highlighted area). The Amarna Letters contain many names of deities, providing us with a catalogue of the gods worshiped in the ancient Near East.

adjective 'Ibrî (Hebrew) found in the oldest texts of the Hebrew Bible, particularly in the Pentateuch (Genesis 14:13, 39:14,17, 40:15, 41:12, 43:32; Exodus 1:15-16,19, 2:6,7,11,13, 3:18, 5:3, 7:16, 9:1, 21:2; Deuteronomy 15:12) but also in 1 Samuel (4:6,9, 13:3,7,19, 14:11,21 and 29:3). Since the patriarch Abraham himself is described as 'Ibrî (Genesis 14:13), it appears that Habiru religion is partially reflected in the oldest patriarchal biblical traditions, those which imply that the groups related to the patriarchs had no knowledge of YHWH (Yahweh).[4]

The groups that would later form biblical Israel at first seem to have worshiped the "god of the father," that is, a family or clan god that eventually became associated with local sanctuaries near which the clan settled. The god sometimes had its own name, but generally it was indicated by a name incorporating the name of the "great god" El or Baal. The traditions surrounding the biblical patriarchs—Abraham, Isaac and Jacob—seem to have been connected to specific geographical areas. Thus from north to south:

1. The Bene-Jacob (Sons of Jacob) probably originated in north-

ern Mesopotamia,[5] the Aramean region around Harran. They probably left this area after the Mittani kingdom—formed by a Hurrian-speaking people in North Syria during the mid-second millennium B.C.E.—was invaded and destroyed by the Assyrians around 1275 B.C.E. The Bene-Jacob settled in the central hill country of what would later become Israel, primarily in the area north and northeast of Shechem.[6] It is possible that this clan took part in the worship at the sanctuary of Baal/El Berit (Master/God of the Alliance) near Shechem (Judges 8:33, 9:4; see also 9:46).[7]

2. The group related to the patriarch Abraham originally settled in the southern Judean mountains around Hebron and its outdoor sanctuary Mamre (Genesis 13:18, 18). In the Bible, Abraham buries Sarah "in the cave of the field of Machpelah facing Mamre (that is, Hebron) in the land of Canaan" (Genesis 23:19). Abraham is also connected to traditions concerning Lot and the southern Dead Sea area (Genesis 13:5-13; 18-19). The old traditions associate Abraham with "El," a word that means "god" but may sometimes refer to a specific Canaanite god named El.[8] Specifically, Abraham's god is variously called "El Shaddai" or "El Elyon" (Genesis 17:1, 14:18-22, 28:3, 35:11, 43:14; Ezekiel 10:5; see also Numbers 24:16; Deuteronomy 26:19, 28:1, 32:8; Psalms 7:18, 9:3, 21:7). In Genesis 17:1, for example, Abraham's god appears before him and says, "I am El Shaddai"; "El Shaddai" is often translated as "God Almighty" but it might also mean "Mountain God."[9] In Genesis 14:19 King Melchizedek of Salem (Jerusalem) says that Abraham is blessed "by El Elyon," which is often translated as "God Most High."[10]

3. The group connected (or related) to the patriarch Isaac apparently lived in the Negev around Beersheba, an area often mentioned as the territory of the tribe of Simeon. The principal sanctuary of this group seems to have been at Beersheba, dedicated to El Olam (Genesis 21:33), often translated as "Eternal God." A

sanctuary farther south was dedicated to El Roi, often translated as "God of Seeing" or "God Who Sees Me" (Genesis 16:13-14).

In all of these instances, the patriarchal groups appear to have worshiped their ancestral gods in local sanctuaries of the gods Baal or El. These sanctuaries are open to the sky, and they all comprise three main elements: an altar, a stela (or standing stone) and a sacred tree.[11]

Thus Abraham builds open altars at the "oak of Moreh" near Shechem (Genesis 12:7) and at the "oaks of Mamre, which are at Hebron" (Genesis 13:18). Isaac builds a similar open altar at Beersheba (Genesis 26:25), as does Jacob at Shechem (Genesis 33:20) and Bethel (Genesis 35:1,3,7).

Jacob erects stelae, or sacred standing stones, in the sanctuary of Bethel (Genesis 28:18,22, 31:13, 35:14) and in Gilead (Genesis 31:45). Other stelae are later erected by Moses, when he builds an altar at the foot of the mountain (Exodus 24:4), and by Joshua, who sets up a "great stone" in Shechem (Joshua 24:26).

The sacred tree could be an oak, as at Mamre (Genesis 13:18, 14:13, 18:1), Moreh (Genesis 12:6; Deuteronomy 11:30) and Bethel (Genesis 35:8); a tamarisk, which Abraham plants near Beersheba (Genesis 21:33); a terebinth-tree, as at Shechem (Genesis 35:4; see also 12:6; Joshua 24:26); or any green tree, to serve as a symbol of power and life.

The patriarchal narratives reflect historical conditions before 1000 B.C.E., the beginning of King David's reign from Hebron.[12] We thus cannot give a detailed history of the Habiru/'Ibrîm religion of Canaan from the 14th century to the tenth century B.C.E. Religious rites, however, are often preserved over long periods of time, and it seems likely that the religious-historical conditions before 1000 B.C.E. had been in effect for generations, perhaps even back to the references to the Habiru in the Amarna Letters (mid-14th century B.C.E.).

Nonetheless, the patriarchal traditions probably reflect the religious situation of the central hill country of Israel just before the arrival of Yahwism. Yahwism did not appear everywhere at the same time: It probably appeared a little before 1200 B.C.E. in the central region, the territory of the tribe of Ephraim, and only about the year 1000 B.C.E. in the mountains of Judah, to the south. Still, even when Yahwism began to spread in these areas, it had to coexist for a time with the traditional religion of the local sanctuaries, so that aspects of this pre-Yahwistic religion of the patriarchal traditions probably remained in effect until the eighth century B.C.E.

The broad outlines of pre-Yahwistic religion in Palestine seem clear enough. High Canaanite society, in more urban areas and in areas with direct contact with Egypt, practiced polytheism, complete with temples of the gods and divine images. On the other hand, clans or tribes in more rural areas practiced a religion based on worship of the "god of the fathers" in various local sanctuaries, particularly sanctuaries dedicated to forms of the god El.

CHAPTER 2

The Origins of Yahwism

The two earliest West Semitic inscriptions referring to YHWH both date to the second half of the ninth century B.C.E. The 4-foot-high Mesha Stela (also called the Moabite Stone) was inscribed with 34 lines of text by Mesha, king of the land of Moab (directly east of the Dead Sea),[1] who tells us that he liberated Moab from the oppression of the Israelite kings Omri (c. 882-871 B.C.E.) and Ahab (c. 871-852 B.C.E.). Line 18 mentions cultic objects of "YHWH" during the Israelite occupation of Nebo.

The Tel Dan Stela, which was found at Tel Dan, north of the Sea of Galilee, also tells of victories over Israelite kings, this time probably by an Aramean king of Damascus named Hazael;[2] line 9 of the Tel Dan Stela identifies one of the defeated Israelite kings as "(Ahaz)iahu" (c. 841 B.C.E.), a name that ends with a Yahwist theophoric element ("YH(W)" in Hebrew).[3] Thus the first epigraphical evidence of YHWH shows him clearly associated with Hebrew kingdoms.

The 14th-century B.C.E. Amarna Letters do not mention such a deity, either directly or as a theophoric element in a personal name or place-name.[4] The epigraphical evidence suggests, then, that YHWH appeared in the land that would become Israel sometime between the mid-14th

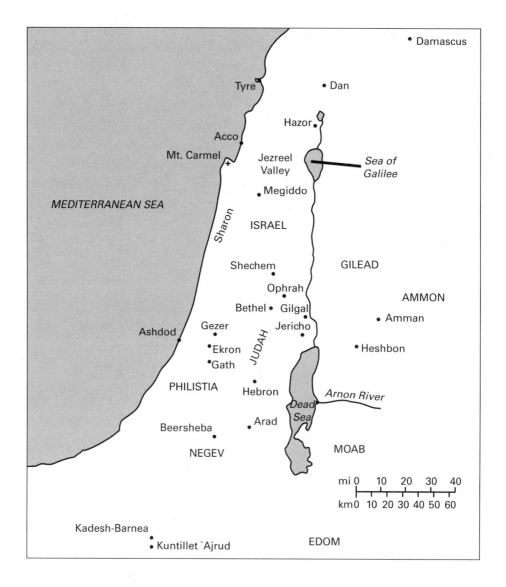

century B.C.E. and the end of the ninth century B.C.E. By the time YHWH does appear in the land, at least in the epigraphical record, he is already a significant figure to the Hebrew population of both the northern kingdom of Israel and the southern kingdom of Judah.[5]

Although archaeology is silent on the origins of Yahwism, the Bible is a rich source of information. The oldest biblical texts are practically unanimous on two significant points: The divine name, the tetragrammaton

(Greek for "four letters," in this case four Hebrew consonants) "YHWH," goes back to Moses; and YHWH, at least to some extent, was brought into Canaan by the group Moses led, the Bene-Israel (Sons of Israel).

The southern origin of Yahwism is indicated not only by stories in the Book of Exodus but also by several very old biblical poems. Thus "YHWH came from Sinai, and dawned from Seir upon us; he shone forth from Mount Paran" (Deuteronomy 33:2); "YHWH, when you went out from Seir, when you marched from the region of Edom, the earth trembled, and the heavens poured, the clouds indeed poured water. The mountains quaked before YHWH, the One of Sinai" (Judges 5:4-5); "God came from Teman, the Holy One from Mount Paran ... I saw the tents of Cushan under affliction; the tent curtains of the land of Midian trembled" (Habakkuk 3:3,7); "O God, when you went out before your people, when you marched through the wilderness, the earth quaked, the heavens poured down rain at the presence of God, the God of Sinai, at the presence of God, the God of Israel" (Psalm 68:7-8).

Even though most of these poems were probably written down during the First Temple period (tenth to early sixth centuries B.C.E.), they show a clear unanimity about the southern origins of YHWH.[6] All the place-names mentioned in these poems are associated with the desert area south of Israel.

Sinai is both a desert (Exodus 19:1; Leviticus 7:38; Numbers 1:1) and a mountain (Exodus 19:11,18,20). Its precise location remains much debated, though most scholars agree that biblical Sinai is near Egypt in the desert area between Egypt and Israel. The use of the term "Sinai" seems characteristic of Judahite (southern) traditions, while Israelite (northern) traditions use the place-name "Horeb" (see 1 Kings 19:8).

Seir is a mountain, or a mountainous country, and the dwelling place of the Bene-Esau (Genesis 36:8; Deuteronomy 2:4,22). Since the name "Esau" ends with the letter *waw*, which seems to connect it to North Arabic names, Seir is probably the mountainous zone south of the Negev.[7] This place-name is attested several times in inscriptions of the Egyptian pharaohs Ramesses II (c. 1279-1213 B.C.E.) and Ramesses III (c. 1187-1156 B.C.E.).[8] Because the Egyptians apparently did not penetrate into the mountains of Edom east of the 'Aravah (the valley extending from the Dead Sea to Gulf of Aqaba), Seir was likely located in the southern Negev or northeastern Sinai, west of the 'Aravah.

Paran is both a desert (Numbers 10:12, 12:16, 13:3) and a mountain (Deuteronomy 33:2). It was apparently inhabited by the Bene-Ishmael (Genesis 21:21) and located close to Kadesh-Barnea (Numbers 13:26), about 50 miles southwest of Beersheba. It appears to have been contiguous with the land of Midian (1 Kings 11:18), though somewhat closer to Egypt. It was thus probably located west or northwest of Kadesh-Barnea.

Although Edom is identified with Seir in the Bible (Genesis 36:1-8,19-20), this tradition probably only goes back to the second half of the eighth century B.C.E., when Edomites crossed the 'Aravah and seized Eilat and the desert zone in the southern Negev (2 Kings 16:6). Before this time, Edom probably designated the mountains east of the 'Aravah. Edom is mentioned once in Papyrus Anastasi VI (lines 54-56), which was composed under Pharaoh Merneptah (c. 1212-1202 B.C.E.). The text, which consists of a dispatch from a border post, suggests only that Edom lay east of the Nile Delta: "We finished letting the Shosu clans of Edom pass the fortress of 'Merneptah-hotep-her-Maat—life, prosperity, health'—which is in Tjeku, to the pools of Per-Atum [perhaps biblical Pithom] ... to maintain them in life and to maintain their herds in life."[9]

Etymologically, Teman means "south" and seems to designate a clan or tribe attached to the Bene-Esau (Genesis 36:11,15,42) and to Edom (Amos 1:12; Jeremiah 49:7). A group of eighth-century B.C.E. paleo-Hebrew inscriptions found at Kuntillet 'Ajrud,[10] in the southern Negev about 40 miles northwest of Eilat, refer to "YHWH of Teman" and "YHWH of Samaria." These phrases are part of traditional blessing formulas used at the beginnings of letters; the phrase "YHWH of Samaria" indicates a letter sent from Samaria (the capital of the northern kingdom of Israel), while the phrase "YHWH of Teman" indicates a letter to be sent from Teman, or Kuntillet 'Ajrud.[11] The region of Teman thus included the site of Kuntillet 'Ajrud.

Cushan is a place-name attested only in Habakkuk 3:7 and its location remains unknown, though it may have been a clan or tribe of Midian (or Midian may have been a clan or tribe of Cushan). This would explain the fact that Aaron and Miriam reproach their brother, Moses, for marrying a "Cushite" woman (Numbers 12:1), whereas Exodus 2:21 clearly states that Moses married Zipporah, the daughter of a priest of Midian. So the wife of Moses is sometimes designated as Midianite and sometimes Cushite (probably an ethnic adjective from "Cushan").

Midian seems to have been a North Arabic country/people. According to the Bible, the Midianites carried on a slave trade with Egypt (Genesis 37:36), perhaps even conducting raids north into what would become the Land of Israel. The last reference to a historical Midian comes when the Aramaean prince "Hadad" flees through Midian to Egypt after David's conquest (1 Kings 11:18).[12] Some archaeologists connect Midian to the flourishing civilization centered in northern Hejaz, east of the Gulf of Aqaba, from about the thirteenth century B.C.E to the tenth century B.C.E.[13]

Clearly, the biblical evidence suggests that Yahwism arose in the southern Negev or northeastern Sinai. Later, in the first half of the ninth century B.C.E., when the prophet Elijah makes a pilgrimage to Horeb/Sinai (1 Kings 19), his route takes him somewhere south of Beersheba.

Some Egyptian texts also provide fascinating evidence of YHWH's southern origins. An inscription of the Egyptian pharaoh Amenhotep III (c. 1390-1353 B.C.E), found at the Nubian site of Soleb,[14] refers to "Shosu of YHW'." (This inscription, a list of routes traveled by the Egyptians, was recopied at the Nubian sites of Amara West[15] and Aksha[16] during the reign of Ramesses II.)[17] This is all the more intriguing in that the phrase "Shosu of YHW'" is parallel to "Shosu of Seir" or "Shosu of the mountain of Seir," attested in the inscriptions of Ramesses II.[18] (Seir, as we have seen, is one of the biblical place-names associated with the origins of YHWH; and "Shosu" refers to a southern nomadic or seminomadic people whom Egypt had trouble controlling). Although "YHW'" in Amenhotep III's route list is a place-name, it is almost certainly related to the divine name YHWH.[19]

What can we say about the historical contexts of the origins of Yahwism?

In the biblical text, the divine name is revealed to Moses. Moreover, Moses' family line remained centrally important for the introduction of Yahwism into Israel and the subsequent continuity of Yahwistic traditions. Consider, for example, the role of the "Aaronide" sacerdotal family (priestly families were descendants of Moses' brother Aaron) at the Shiloh sanctuary. This sanctuary, in the heart of Israel's central hill country, was probably the principal Yahwist sanctuary prior to the rise of the monarchy; it was also a pilgrimage center (Judges 21:19; 1 Samuel 1:3,21) and home of the Ark of the Covenant, the central symbol of the Israelite armies since the 11th century B.C.E. (1 Samuel 4:3ff.) and the embodiment of Israel's covenant with YHWH. The priests of the Shiloh sanctuary were descendants of the priest Eli, and they are called "Elides."[20]

One of David's staunchest allies and closest friends, Abiathar (1 Samuel 22:20ff. to 1 Kings 2:26-27), was a descendant of the Elide sacerdotal family. This suggests that the writing down of the old Mosaic traditions, in the early tenth century, involved the use of material transmitted from Shiloh. This would also explain the diffusion of these old traditions within Israel of the monarchic period.

Not only does Moses receive the revelation of the divine name "YHWH" but his descendants preside over the Yahwist sanctuary at Shiloh, home of the Ark of the Covenant, and sit side-by-side with King David, the father of the Israelite nation, the people of Yahweh.

The problem here is that so much of the Bible—narratives, laws and rites (and the entire Pentateuch)—has been associated with Moses that this central figure tends to disappear under the weight of tradition.[21] Should we, then, relegate all of the biblical material relating to Moses to the realm of legend? I do not think so. As the French scholar Roland de Vaux wrote, "Removing Moses makes the religion and even the existence of Israel inexplicable."[22] Thus we can only try to distinguish what, in the flood of Mosaic traditions, may go back to the historical Moses.

The name "Moses" is Egyptian, and we find it built into such pharaonic names as Ahmose and Thutmose. Moreover, the construction of the towns of Pithom and Ramesses (Exodus 1:11), probably to be identified with Per-Atum/Pithom (Tell el-Maskhuta or Tell el-Retabeh?) and Pi-Ramesses (Tell ed-Dabâ/Qantir),[23] provides a good chronological indicator: the beginning of the very long reign of Ramesses II (c. 1279-1213 B.C.E.).

The biblical text tells us that Moses killed an Egyptian foreman and fled to Midian to escape the Egyptian police. This story, especially Moses' sojourn with the Midianites, seems plausible. As Roland de Vaux observed, later biblical narratives show hostility to the Midianites: for example, the war against Midian as recounted in Numbers 31, and the Midianites' oppression of the Israelites as told in Judges 6-8. Much later, when these stories were being written down, the Midianites were known to have been enemies of the Israelites, so the scribes would not have invented the tradition that Moses married a Midianite woman, or that he received the revelation of YHWH in Midian, or that a Midianite man had played an important role in leading the Israelite people. Moses' marrying a Midianite woman, which arouses the wrath of Aaron and Miriam (Numbers 12:1), and Moses' humble occupation as shepherd of "the flock of his father-in-law Jethro, the priest of Midian" (Exodus 3:1) have a ring of truth. These events, as de Vaux says, "have a historical basis."[24]

It is in this context that biblical tradition places the revela-

THE MESHA STELA. This 4-foot-high black basalt slab was erected in about 810 B.C.E. by Mesha, king of Moab, to give thanks to the Moabite god Chemosh for delivering his people from Israelite rule and for his conquest of new territories. Line 18 mentions cultic objects of "YHWH"–one of the earliest references to the Israelite God.

Z. RADOVAN/WWW.BIBLELANDPICTURES.COM

tion of the divine name to Moses. This revelation takes place in a sacred place—Horeb, "the mountain of God" (Exodus 3:1)—and is directly related to the presence of a "bush," which is the desert equivalent of the sacred tree of traditional sanctuaries. In this Midianite sanctuary, Moses receives the revelation of the divine name in the form of the tetragrammaton YHWH. This deity assigns Moses the mission of leading the Hebrews out of Egypt and into the desert to make offerings to his name (Exodus 3:18).

Given the geographical and historical contexts described above, this revelation and mission appear thoroughly plausible, especially in that they involve a limited number of people: the clan of Moses. If we add the references to "YHW'" in the Egyptian route lists, then we should interpret YHWH as the Midianite "god of their fathers," with Jethro being the priest of the sanctuary where Moses had his revelation.

Once Moses succeeds in leading the Hebrews out of Egypt and into the desert, it is Jethro who presides over the making of offerings to YHWH in the YHWH sanctuary where he is priest (Exodus 18:1-12): "Jethro, Moses' father-in-law, brought a burnt offering and sacrifices to YHWH" (Exodus 18:12). Here, the very first time an offering is made to YHWH, Moses and Aaron play only subordinate roles.[25] This could hardly have been invented later.

What were the characteristics of Midianite YHWH? Once again, the evidence is limited. We have no original Midianite document, and this North Arabic people seems to have disappeared in the tenth century B.C.E. The theonym "YHWH" does not appear in any North Arabic text or personal name of the first millennium B.C.E. Paradoxically, although YHWH seems clearly to have had North Arabic origins, at least according to the biblical traditions, the name survived the disappearance of the Midianites only by becoming the name of the "God of Israel," the principal deity of the kingdoms of Israel and Judah in the first half of the first millennium B.C.E.

YHWH appears to have been the principal deity of those Midianites who lived in the mountainous area of the central Negev. Nothing suggests that Midianite worship of YHWH extended to Midianite populations east of the 'Aravah. It was probably limited to the region of the "mountain of God, Horeb," which in Numbers 10:33 is called the "mountain of YHWH."

Thus YHWH seems to have been a mountain God, a reputation that he still held in the ninth century B.C.E. According to 1 Kings 20:23, the Aramean soldiers tell their king that the Israelite gods are "gods of the hills, and so they were stronger than we."

The blessing pronounced by Jethro refers to other gods: "YHWH is greater than all the gods" (Exodus 18:10-11). This suggests that Midianite Yahwism did not deny the existence of other gods; it simply considered YHWH the greatest of the gods. This is also true, as we shall see, of First Temple Israelite Yahwism. Early Yahwism was not monotheistic.

It is more difficult to say whether early Yahwism was monolatrous. There is no reference to the worship of any other deity by Jethro or Moses; nor is there any mention of the presence or worship of another deity in the sanctuary where Jethro was priest. Moreover, Moses is able to lead his people out of Egypt by making sacrifices "to YHWH, our God," also called the "God of the Hebrews" (Exodus 3:18). Jethro also blesses YHWH for delivering the people from the Egyptians (Exodus 18:10). The biblical evidence suggests that the people of Israel worshiped only YHWH, that early Yahwism was monolatrous—which is given expression in a covenant between YHWH and Israel (Exodus 34:10).

According to Exodus 3:18 and 18:10, worship of YHWH was characterized by prayers, blessings and sacrifices, in particular sacrifices involving a communal meal (Exodus 18:12). According to some stray references, the Yahwistic sanctuary of Horeb seems to have comprised an altar (Exodus 17:15, 24:4), one or several stelae (24:4) (the reference to "twelve" stelae is probably not earlier than the tenth century B.C.E.) and a sacred bush (Exodus 3:2-4; Deuteronomy 33:16). Finally, the YHWH sanctuary seems to have had no statue or representation of the deity. Although this is only an argument from silence, the early worship of YHWH could well have been aniconic.

So YHWH was probably a god worshiped by a Midianite people of North Arabia, and his earliest known sanctuary lay in the southern Negev, in the mountains of the central Negev or in the northeastern part of Sinai. This YHWH cult was at least contemporaneous with Moses, around the reign of Ramesses II (c. 1279-1213 B.C.E.), though it could have gone back to the 14th century B.C.E., given the references to YHW' in the route lists of Amenhotep III (c. 1390-1353 B.C.E.). The adoption of this North Arabic deity by Moses was the consequence of his marriage with the daughter of a Midianite priest and led to the adoption of this deity by the clan of Moses. Early Yahwism seems not to have been monotheistic, as it recognized the existence of other gods, but it does seem to have been monolatrous, as the clan of Moses worshiped no other god. Like other cults dedicated to the "god of the father," early Yahwism apparently consisted of worship within the framework of a sanctuary with an altar, a stela and a sacred bush.[26]

CHAPTER 3

Early Yahwism in Israel's Central Hill Country

The sojourn of the Moses clan with the Midianites in the area of Kadesh-Barnea and the mountains of the central Negev could have involved an increase in population, since the Hebrews had a reputation for being prolific (Exodus 1:7-20). Obtaining food and water probably became increasingly difficult. Despite the kindness of Jethro, economic and demographic factors probably spurred the decision to separate (Exodus 18:27), and so Moses and his people sought more hospitable ground.

According to biblical tradition, they marched east and then north to the Transjordan, circumventing the land of Moab, which lay directly east of the Dead Sea. It seems likely that the Israelites avoided Moab because Egypt continued to be influential among the Moabites.[1]

In the Transjordan, along the northern border of Moab, the Israelites, together with other groups, may have begun to occupy arable sites. They seized the Heshbon area, possibly by force, and camped in "the plains of Moab, in Transjordan, in front of Jericho" (Numbers 22:1; Deuteronomy 34:1). The battle of Heshbon may have marked the beginning of the "wars of YHWH," recorded in a collection of old poems called "the Book of the Wars of YHWH" (Numbers 21:14).[2] It is here that biblical tradition places the death of Moses:

> Then Moses went up from the plains of Moab to Mount Nebo, to the top of Pisgah, which is opposite Jericho, and YHWH showed him the whole land ... YHWH said to him: "This is the land of which I swore to Abraham, to Isaac, and to Jacob, saying, 'I will give it to your descendants'; I have let you see it with your eyes, but you shall not cross over there." Then Moses, the servant of YHWH, died there in the land of Moab, opposite Beth-peor, but no one knows his burial place to this day (Deuteronomy 34:1-6).

The leadership of his group, the Bene-Israel, was then entrusted to one of Moses' military leaders, Joshua (Exodus 17:8-16), the first biblical figure to have a Yahwistic name (Numbers 13:4-16). (The Hebrew form of Joshua, "Yehoshua," begins with the theophoric element "YH(W).") As head of the Bene-Israel, Joshua was to see that his people kept their Yahwist traditions.

Although the biblical Book of Joshua is traditionally thought to be a history of the Israelites' conquering the Holy Land, the account of the conquest seems to have been developed later on, probably at the time of the composition of the so-called Deuteronomistic History during the reigns of the Judahite kings Hezekiah (c. 727-699 B.C.E.) and Josiah (c. 640-609 B.C.E.). (Most scholars believe the Deuteronomistic History—comprising the books of Joshua, Judges, Samuel and Kings—was composed probably using some older sources at the same time as the Book of Deuteronomy; all of these works were re-edited after the Babylonian destruction of the Temple in 587 B.C.E.)

If Joshua's conquest and destruction of numerous cities belongs largely to the realm of legend, the Book of Joshua nonetheless probably preserves some historical material, such as Joshua's treaty with the Gibeonites (Joshua 9) and his battle against a Canaanite coalition at the Beth-Horon ascent (Joshua 10).[3] Moreover, this battle against the Canaanite coalition seems to reflect conditions described in the hieroglyphic text inscribed on the Merneptah Stela (also called the Israel Stela), now in the Cairo Museum.[4] This stela, erected early in the reign of the Egyptian pharaoh Merneptah (c. 1213-1204 B.C.E.),[5] tells of the king's campaigns in Canaan, where he defeated a people called "Israel"—the earliest reference to Israel in the archaeological record. According to both Joshua 10 and the Merneptah Stela, both adversaries claimed victory. (Merneptah stela: "Israel is laid waste"; Joshua 10:10: "He [Joshua] defeated them utterly in Gibeon; he pursued them down the pass of Beth-Horon.") Actually the battle seems to have resulted in the maintenance of the status quo, with the Bene-Israel remaining in the central hill country and the Egyptians deciding to stay out of the area. This provides a valuable chronological reference for the beginnings of Yahwism in Israel.

Moreover, the role of Joshua as a Yahwist warrior seems consistent with later references to YHWH at the head of the armies (or Lord of Hosts), especially in connection with the Yahwist sanctuary of Shiloh, resting place of the Ark of the Covenant (1 Samuel 1:3,11, 4:4).[6]

Joshua's role in the so-called Shechem assembly (see Joshua 24), dating roughly to 1200 B.C.E., is probably also historical. Even though the texts we have were recomposed by various later redactors, an actual historical event was probably the basis of this proposed alliance with Hebrew groups that were not part of the Exodus and thus did not know YHWH. Joshua tells the people to revere YHWH and to "put away the gods that [their] ancestors served beyond the River [that is, the Euphrates River] ... the gods of the Amorites" (Joshua 24:14-15). These were probably the Bene-Jacob who arrived from northern Mesopotamia; Joshua tells them to give up their ancestral god (probably Pahad), the "god of their fathers," and commit themselves to the service of YHWH alone (Joshua 24:23; Genesis 35:2,4).[7]

This alliance then becomes the basis for rallying other groups to the Israelite confederation,[8] with each of these clans/tribes retaining its inheritance (Numbers 36:9):

> Joshua made a covenant with the people that day, and made
> statutes and ordinances for them at Shechem. He took a large
> stone, and set it up there under the oak in the sanctuary of

> YHWH. Joshua said to all the people, "See, this stone shall be a witness against us, for it has heard all the words of YHWH that he spoke to us; therefore it shall be witness against you, if you deal falsely with your God." So Joshua sent the people away to their inheritances (Joshua 24:25-28).

This "constitution" of the Israelite confederation probably consisted of a few basic rules demanding mutual respect among the members of the alliance and laying out the consequences for violating these rules. They could have constituted an early form of the Decalogue, which probably did not receive its final form until after the Exile (sixth century B.C.E.).[9] The most important rule of course, is the commandment to worship only YHWH. And all this takes place in an open-air sanctuary devoted to YHWH, replete with stela and sacred tree. In telling the Israelites to give up their ancestral gods, Joshua implicitly recognized the existence—if not the power—of those gods, thus giving expression to a monolatrous (not monotheistic) Yahwism.

In becoming the official religion of the confederation, Yahwism ensured a core of cultural and religious unity among the various Habiru/Ibrîm groups (Benjamin, Ephraim and Manasseh in the central hill country; Gilead and other groups in the Transjordan; and various groups in Galilee), which, gradually and step by step, came to form Israel.

Each of these clans/tribes may have continued to worship at its local sanctuary: at Gilgal, Shechem, Bethel, Ophrah, Dan and so on. This picture is consistent with the archaeological record. For example, one such local sanctuary has been uncovered on a hill north of Shechem (at Dhaharat-Tawilah), where archaeologists found a small bronze Canaanite bull dated to about the 12th century B.C.E.;[10] however, there is no indication of the name of the deity to which this sanctuary was dedicated. What may be an Iron Age I (1200-1000 B.C.E.) sanctuary with a large altar has been found on Mount Ebal by the Israeli archaeologist Adam Zertal,[11] though the interpretation of the site is much debated.

Perhaps the most authentic representative of Israelite Yahwism is the Shiloh sanctuary in the territory of Ephraim,[12] the tribe of Joshua. Shiloh has been identified as modern Tell Seilun, about 17 miles north of

BRONZE BULL. This 4-inch-high and 7-inch-long figurine dates to the 12th-century B.C.E. and was found at an Israelite site near Biblical Dothan, in Samaria. The Canaanite god El was often called a bull; this object suggests that early Israelite religion was greatly influenced by Canaanite worship.

Bethel. This site has been excavated several times, most recently in the 1980s under the direction of Israeli archaeologist Israel Finkelstein. Although the Shiloh excavations have not revealed the remains of any Iron Age I sanctuary (leaving open the possibility that the early Yahwist sanctuary at Shiloh was an open-air precinct), the archaeologists have found 26 Iron Age I sites within a radius of only a few miles,[13] which suggests the demographic importance of the region of Shiloh after the time of Joshua.

The early biblical texts make several references to an annual pilgrimage festival celebrated at Shiloh (Judges 21:19; 1 Samuel 1:3,21), which seems to have been an important gathering point for all the peoples of the central hill country. According to biblical tradition, Shiloh was home to the Ark of the Covenant, the symbol of the power of the Israelite armies (1 Samuel 4:3; cf. Joshua 3-4, 6; 2 Samuel 11:11). The ark was guarded by the sacerdotal dynasty of the Elides (descendants of Eli), who were connected to the Aaronide priesthood and Exodus traditions; the names of the two sons of Eli, Hophni and Phinehas (1 Samuel 4:4), are Egyptian names. Thus Shiloh is extremely important in the development and diffusion of Yahwism.

Even though the Shiloh sanctuary may well have been destroyed by the Philistines in the mid-11th century B.C.E. (see 1 Samuel 4:1ff.), the Mosaic Yahwism of the Elide tradition continued to be influential in Israel—initially because of the important role played by the prophet Samuel, who was trained at Shiloh (1 Samuel 3:20ff.); and later because of the role played by Abiathar son of Ahimelech (1 Samuel 23:6), son of Ahituv (1 Samuel 22:9), brother of Ikabod, son of Phinehas, son of Eli (1 Samuel 14:3; see also 4:21). The Elide priest Abiathar served as David's companion and as priest of the Israelite nation during David's reigns in Hebron and in Jerusalem, though he was dismissed by David's son and successor, Solomon (1 Kings 2:26-27). Through Samuel and Abiathar, Yahwism spread among the Israelite people.

The religious history of the Israelite confederation is known to us principally through the Bible (with some help from the Merneptah Stela). The main sources of information, the books of Joshua and Judges, did not reach their final form until, at the earliest, the reign of the Judahite king Josiah and the influence of the Deuteronomistic party in the seventh century B.C.E. Nonetheless, these biblical sources convey material that does not correspond to the religious ideology of the seventh century—such as the significance of the sanctuaries at Shechem and Shiloh, and the legislative power attached to Joshua. It is likely, then, that this material was partly transmitted in some written form and retained because the biblical authors believed it really happened. This history reveals the important role played by the Elide priesthood even if, by the seventh century B.C.E., it had long been supplanted by the Zadokite dynasty.

CHAPTER 4
YHWH the God of Israel

The defeat of the Israelite army by the Philistines (1 Samuel 4:1ff.) resulted in the destruction of the Shiloh sanctuary and the Philistines' capture of the Ark of the Covenant, the symbol of the presence of YHWH at the head of the Israelite armies. To a certain extent, the battle between the Israelites and Philistines led to a confrontation between YHWH, "God of Israel," and Dagon, the principal god of the Philistines.[1] The story told in 1 Samuel 5—in which the Ark of the Covenant is installed in the Philistine cities of Ashdod, Gath and Ekron, causing much damage to the local sanctuaries and populations—is probably an attempt to recover some dignity from the Israelites' defeat.

The Philistine threat forced the Israelites to choose a leader able to carry out a war of liberation from the Philistine yoke. That became the task of Saul, Israel's first king, and the war with the Philistines tragically consumed "all the days of Saul" (1 Samuel 14:52). Saul died during the battle on Mount Gilboa (1 Samuel 31); the Philistines placed his weapons as offerings in a temple (or in several temples) of Astarte and they nailed his corpse to a wall in Beth-Shean (1 Samuel 31:10). Israel and Yahwism seemed about to disappear, absorbed into Philistine civilization.

It is in this context that David rose to power as the Israelite king in Hebron (c. 1010-1003 B.C.E.) and Jerusalem (c. 1003-970 B.C.E.). Some versions of this story, told in the books of Samuel, were probably first composed by a descendant of Shiloh's Elide priesthood, Abiathar, or a scirbe of his circle. This scribe has been rightly called Israel's "first historian."[2] The antiquity of the story, however, does not mean that it presents a balanced and critical view, what we today call "history." The account of David's rise to power is largely propaganda, designed to present him as the legitimate king of all Israel even though he did not descend from Saul.[3]

Among the numerous political assassinations that David supposedly ordered and the various dynastic marriages he is said to have entered,[4] one aspect of these stories probably has a historical basis: David was a supporter of YHWH. This was useful to him when he was recognized as king by the elders of Israel in Hebron (2 Samuel 5:1-3). YHWH "was with him" (1 Samuel 16:12,13, 17:37, 18:12,28, 20:13) because David led the "YHWH wars" (1 Samuel 18:17, 25:28).[5]

The fact that David was a passionate supporter of YHWH explains why his reign was marked by a significant expansion of Yahwism. This expansion has four principal aspects:

1. David was initially proclaimed king of Judah in Hebron (1 Samuel 2:1-4). Hebron lies in the south, about midway between Jerusalem and Beersheba. Hebron, that is, lies at the center of the territory that would become the Judahite kingdom. But this territory did not form part the Israelite confederation prior to the emergence of David;[6] indeed, nothing indicates that YHWH was then known in the Jerusalem-Hebron-Beersheba corridor. From the time of David on, however, Yahwism was the official religion of this Judahite area.

2. After defeating the Philistines, David extended his power in Canaanite zones that had been under Philistine influence: the plains of Jezreel, Sharon and Akko. This political domination was probably accompanied by a diffusion of the official Yahwistic

worship, even if local culture and religion were not given up immediately.

3. Once David made Jerusalem the capital of the unified Israelite kingdom, consisting of the territories that would later become the southern kingdom of Judah and the northern kingdom of Israel, he sought to make Jerusalem the Israelite religious capital as well. He thus organized a ceremony in which the Ark of the Covenant was installed in Jerusalem (2 Samuel 6). With this symbol of YHWH at the head of the Israelite armies, and with the help of the Elide priest Abiathar, David transferred the principal center of Yahwistic worship from Shiloh to Jerusalem.

4. The reign of David probably marks the true birth of Hebrew literature as the propagandistic arm of the new kingship. As we have seen, the history of David's ascent to power was likely written by a scribe (or group of scribes) of Abiathar to present David as the legitimate king of Judah and, later, of all Israel. This scribe (or group of scribes) may also have been responsible for writing down the patriarchal traditions, which place great emphasis on Abraham: The role of the patriarch Abraham as ancestor of the Hebrews corresponds to some extent with that of David as head of the unified kingdom.[7]

This expansion of the state and the state religion, Yahwism, also posed a problem. What happened when Yahwism reached into areas where it was hitherto unknown, encountering the traditional forms of worship in these new territories? Were the local gods to be utterly rejected in favor of the exclusive worship of YHWH, as had been proposed by Joshua at the Shechem assembly? Wouldn't any forced religious unification cause only anger and resentment, posing an obstacle to political unification?

The genius of David and his allies was to avoid the extreme Joshua-like rhetoric concerning the exclusive worship of YHWH and to propose, instead, that the various "patriarchal" religious traditions be integrated within Yahwism. The deity, though called by different names, was

MOUNT GILBOA. Saul, Israel's first king, was killed here while fighting the Philistines, who made offerings to the goddess Astarte of his weapons. Had it not been for the rise of David, the Israelites might have disappeared within Philistine culture.

always the same supreme Deity; the various versions of the god El in the numerous sanctuaries of the unified kingdom—whether attached to Abraham, Isaac or Jacob—ultimately represented the same great God, who was known as YHWH to the Israelites. This is clearly stated in the passage from Exodus in which God reveals his divine name to Moses:

> I am the God of your father, the God of Abraham, the God of Isaac, the God of Jacob ... Thus you shall say to the Israelites: YHWH, the God of your ancestors, the God of Abraham, the God of Isaac, and the God of Jacob, has sent me to you. This is my name forever, and this my title for all generations (Exodus 3:6-15).

Such a policy of assimilation made it possible for various peoples to keep alive their sanctuaries and ancestral traditions while coating them with the varnish of Yahwism.

David's integration of various local cults of the god El into Yahwism began a process in which Yahwism was transformed from within.[8] Little by little, YHWH took on the features and functions attributed by the local population and Canaanite culture to the supreme god El: YHWH was the creator, He was eternal, He was a warrior, He was the ultimate source of wisdom. According to Roland de Vaux: "This assimilation of Yahweh with El had been prepared by that of the god of the father with El, and it was done without a fight: There is no trace of a conflict between Yahweh and El. Yahweh took from El his character of cosmic God and the title of king."[9]

The enrichment of the attributes of YHWH—originally the mountain God, the warrior God and, perhaps, the storm God—occurred gradually over time. Although the assimilation of traditional local forms of worship (as opposed to Joshua's command to "put away the gods" of the "ancestors") was in place early in David's reign, it was a process that would continue until the reform of King Hezekiah at the end of the eighth century B.C.E.[10]

Consider one example, Abraham's meeting with Melchizedek in Genesis 14:

King Melchizedek of Salem [Jerusalem] brought out bread and wine; he was priest of God Most High [El Elyon]. He blessed him and said, "Blessed be Abram by God Most High, maker of heaven and earth; and blessed be God Most High, who has delivered your enemies into your hands." And Abram gave him one tenth of everything. Then the king of Sodom said to Abram, "Give me the persons, but take the goods for yourself." But Abram said to the king of Sodom, "I have sworn to YHWH, God Most High [El Elyon], maker of heaven and earth, that I would not take a thread or a sandal-thong or anything that is yours, so that you might not say, 'I have made Abram rich'" (Genesis 14: 18-23).

This account may well have been written during the reign of David in Jerusalem.[11] Melchizedek is described as being not only the king of Salem (Jerusalem) but also the priest of El Elyon (often translated "God

Most High"); he uses this divine name twice in his blessing, and he even refers to *El Elyon* as "maker of heaven and earth." Finally YHWH himself is referred to as *El Elyon* and maker of heaven and earth.

References to *El Elyon* also appear in the archaeological record. A blessing formula on an eighth-century B.C.E. Aramaic inscription from the Syrian site of Sfire mentions "El and '*Elyân* ... Heaven and Earth" (I A, 11-12).[12] The first part of Melchizedek's blessing—"*El* ... maker of ... earth"—is also clearly attested in a Phoenician inscription (A III, 18) from Karatepe (in south-central Turkey), dating around 700 B.C.E.[13] Finally, a fragmentary inscription probably reading "[El], creator of earth" appears on an earthenware jar—dating roughly to the second half of the eighth century B.C.E.—that was found in Jerusalem.[14] This inscription and the passage on Melchizedek[15] seem to suggest that worship of *El Elyon* was rooted in the city of Jerusalem, probably before it was captured by David.

Interestingly, the final reference to *El Elyon* in the Melchizedek passage is clearly identified with YHWH: "I have sworn to YHWH, God Most High [*El Elyon*], maker of heaven and earth." In the Psalms, too, the word *Elyon* is often used as a qualifier for YHWH (Psalms 7:17, 9:2, 21:7).

YHWH and *El Elyon* are then completely assimilated, and henceforth YHWH is recognized explicitly as a creator God.[16] Thus the creation account attributed to J (the "Yahwist" creation account, probably written in Jerusalem although its date is disputed) describes "the day that YHWH God made the earth and the heavens" (Genesis 2:4). (Scholars have discerned four main narrative strands in the Torah/Pentateuch: one in which, from the beginning, God is called YHWH [J, from the German spelling of "Yahweh"], one in which God is called Elohim [E], one put together by the author/redactor of Deuteronomy [D], and one created or edited by a Priestly School [P].)

This integration of diverse forms of worship into Yahwism meant that YHWH absorbed the attributes of other great gods. This is a significant evolution. Not only does it testify to the increasing significance of YHWH,[17] but it also shows that YHWH, in taking on the attributes of other gods—in particular, those of El as creator, healer and source of wisdom—would gradually render those other gods unnecessary and useless. In other words, little by little, YHWH penetrated all levels of the Israelite society and became the sole "God of Israel."

Yahwism's infiltration into the "new" territories took place slowly. Even among David's partisans, the number of personal names with the Yahwist theophoric -yah(u) remains small (the frequency of such names, however, is not always a sign of the popularity of the cult). Of David's sons, only the fourth (Adonijah) and fifth (Shephatiah) have Yahwist names ending with the Hebrew "YH" (see 2 Samuel 3:4), and none of his sons born in Jerusalem (2 Samuel 5:14-16) has a Yahwist name.[18] Yahwist names are somewhat more common among David's senior officials (2 Samuel 8:16-18, 20:23-25), though one finds only two such names among the "thirty-seven" officers of David (Benaiah and Uriah [2 Samuel 23:30-39]).[19] This situation remains about the same in the time of Solomon (see 1 Kings 4).

The reign of Solomon is marked especially by the construction of the Jerusalem Temple (1 Kings 6-9:9), officially confirming Jerusalem as the center of Yahwism. This was a new element in the Yahwist tradition; before this, YHWH did not have a house of stone but, at most, a tent (2 Samuel 7:6). The Temple was built, however, according to Canaanite tradition (see the construction of the Baal temple in the Ugaritic texts); specifically, it was built on a Canaanite Phoenician plan with the technical assistance of Hiram, king of Tyre. (Archaeologically, nothing has survived of the Jerusalem Temple, except possibly the base of the eastern retaining wall of the Temple Mount. The site itself is of course unavailable to archaeologists.)[20] Moreover, the Jerusalem Temple seems to have been a kind of royal chapel attached to the royal palace and therefore narrowly controlled by the sovereign.[21] One notes that in the description of the Temple and its furnishings, there is no mention of a statue or representation of YHWH; Yahwism retained its aniconism.

According to the Bible, Solomon was also responsible for other, non-Yahwistic religious structures. For example, he constructed a "high place" (bāmāh) for the worship of the Moabite god Chemosh as well as a sanctuary for the Ammonite god Milkom/Molech on a hill east of Jerusalem (1 Kings 11:5.7). These sanctuaries were constructed not for the local population but for foreign princesses or officials from Transjordan. Still, as the sanctuaries were under the protection of the king, they constituted a temptation for the local population and could throw some doubt on the exclusive character of YHWH worship for Israel. More generally, this situation suggests that the Yahwism of Solomon was not monotheistic and could exist comfortably in a polytheistic—or henotheistic—environment.

CHAPTER 5

Yahwism of the First Temple Period: Monotheism or Monolatry?

W as early Yahwism monotheistic or polytheistic? In fact, this question is not terribly meaningful for the Yahwism of the early part of the First Temple period (tenth to early sixth century B.C.E., when the Temple was destroyed by the Babylonians). The Yahwism of this time was not primarily the fruit of philosophical or theological reflection, or of a theoretical conception of the divine world, but rather a practical religion expressing itself, in particular, in worship and in law.

In the general polytheistic context of the ancient Near East, the early biblical tradition stresses that YHWH was the exclusive national deity of the people of Israel: The Israelites were to worship no other god. At first glance, two fundamental texts of the early religious tradition, going back at least to the First Temple period, seem to reveal a thoroughly monotheistic Yahwism:

I am YHWH your God, who brought you out of the land of Egypt, out of the house of slavery; you shall have no other gods before me. You shall not make yourself an idol, whether in the form of anything that is in heaven above, or that is on the earth beneath, or that is in the water under the earth. You shall not bow down to them or worship them (Exodus 20:2-4; Deuteronomy 5:6-9).

Hear, O Israel: YHWH is our God, YHWH alone (Deuteronomy 6:4).

Looking more closely at these texts, however, one realizes that the first text, taken literally, does not deny the existence of other gods. It demands only that the people of Israel worship only YHWH. In other words, there may be a number of gods, but the people of Israel are restricted to worshiping only one of them, YHWH. This text, then, may well express a form of monolatry, not a universal monotheism. What is emphasized is the special bond between YHWH and Israel, leaving open the possibility that other nations should worship other gods. The second text, too, states that YHWH and only YHWH is the god of Israel.[1]

Other early biblical texts present YHWH, God of Israel, as belonging to an assembly of gods, to a kind of pantheon, which at least apparently implies some form of polytheism. Thus "God has taken his place in the divine council; in the midst of the gods he holds judgment" (Psalm 82:1). And this,

Let the heavens praise your wonders, O YHWH,
your faithfulness in the assembly of the holy ones.
For who in the skies can be compared to YHWH?
Who among the heavenly beings is like YHWH,
a God feared in the council of the holy ones
great and awesome above all that are around him?
(Psalm 89:5-7).

The Book of Job, too, tells us, "One day the heavenly beings came to present themselves before YHWH" (Job 1:6, 2:1; see also Job 38:7 and Psalm 29:1).

Other texts state clearly that while YHWH is the God of Israel other nations have other gods: "When the Most High [*Elyon*] apportioned the nations, when he divided humankind, he fixed the boundaries of the peoples according to the number of the sons of god" (Deuteronomy 32:8). Later expositors were offended by this reference to other gods and emended the traditional Jewish text (Masoretic text) to read "sons of Israel" instead of "the number of the sons of god." However, the Dead Sea Scrolls (and the Greek translation known as the Septuagint) have preserved the original reading.[2] According to the Book of Micah, "[A]ll the peoples walk, each in the name of its god; but we will walk in the name of YHWH our God, forever and ever" (Micah 4:5).

These texts indicate that each of the peoples in the biblical world had its own god, its own national deity. YHWH is the "God of Israel" (Genesis 33:20; Exodus 5:1; 24:10), and the people of Israel are the "people

ERICH LESSING

WIELDING A SPEAR, the figure on this 40-inch-high basalt stela is thought to represent Chemosh, the god of the Moabites. Author André Lemaire notes that it was common in the ancient Near East for some people to worship their national god even while acknowledging that other peoples had their own deities.

of YHWH" (Numbers 11:29, 17:6; Judges 5:11). This special and exclusive bond is wonderfully expressed by images of marriage and, especially, by the idea of a "covenant," or official contractual alliance, between YHWH and Israel.[3] This is also why we often find YHWH called a "jealous" God, for the people of Israel are prohibited from serving other, foreign gods and must serve only him.[4]

If the Israelites were monolatrous, restricted to worshiping only YHWH, were other peoples in the region monolatrous as well? We cannot say for certain, but it does appear that similar forms of monolatry may have been practiced by some of Israel's neighbors—especially the Ammonite, Moabite and Edomite kingdoms of Transjordan.[5]

Our knowledge of religious worship in the Ammonite kingdom during the First Temple period is rather uncertain. There are numerous attestations of El (God), and "Milkom" seems to be the name of a god especially worshiped by the Ammonites. Very possibly, then, Milkom was one of the forms of El (as early on YHWH was one of the forms of El) and Ammonite religion was a monolatrous religion devoted to the god Milkom. Although we know even less about the Edomites, the information we have suggests that they were also monolatrous. Inscriptions from the latter part of the First Temple period reveal that the "national" Edomite god was called Qôs (not mentioned in the Bible), as attested by the first-century C.E. historian Flavius Josephus (*Jewish Antiquities* 15.253)[6] and now by numerous fourth century B.C.E. Aramaic ostraca from Idumea.

The religious situation of the Moabite kingdom is somewhat better known. According to the Bible, the "god of Moab" was called Chemosh (1 Kings 11:33) and the Moabites were the "people of Chemosh" (Numbers 21:29; Jeremiah 48:46). The special bond between Chemosh and Moab seems to be confirmed by epigraphy. According to the ninth-century B.C.E. Mesha Stela (or Moabite Stone), the people of Chemosh and the people of Moab are the same. Lines 11 and 12 of the stela read, "And I killed all the population and the city belonged to Chemosh and Moab."[7] Moreover, Chemosh seems, like YHWH, the national god who leads the armies of his people: "And Chemosh said to me: 'Go, take Nebo from Israel'" (Mesha Stela, line 14).

According to the Mesha Stela, the expansion of Moabite power north of the Arnon River resulted in a systematic destruction of Yahwist sanctuaries and the construction of new sanctuaries dedicated to Chemosh. Because of the monolatrous character of the two national religions (Moabite and Israelite), the worship of YHWH, mentioned several times on the stela, could not continue to be practiced in the territory of Moab and had to be replaced by the exclusive worship of Chemosh. Chemosh's role as the Moabite national deity is also confirmed by numerous references to him in Moabite inscriptions, mainly on seals and seal-impressions.[8]

The early biblical tradition indicates that the Yahwism of the First Temple period in Israel was monolatrous, not monotheistic.[9] It also seems clear, especially from the evidence of the Mesha Stela, that the Israelites shared this kind of religious practice with several neighboring peoples, in particular the Moabites.

CHAPTER 6

The Divided Kingdom and the Resurgence of Baalism

The so-called "Shechem schism" (1 Kings 12:1-19)—the rebellion of one of King Solomon's former officials, Jeroboam, against Solomon's son and successor, Rehoboam—led to the separation of the two "houses" of Israel. Rehoboam (c. 931-914 B.C.E.) became the first king of the separated southern kingdom of Judah, and Jeroboam (c. 931-910 B.C.E.) became the first king of the northern kingdom of Israel. The first 50 years of the divided kingdom were marked by a border war, two foreign invasions—by the Egyptian pharaoh Shoshenq I (c. 945-925 B.C.E.), called Shishak in the Bible (1 Kings 14:25-28), and King Bar-Hadad of Damascus (1 Kings 15:18-20)—and several *coups d'état* in the northern kingdom. The political situation improved only with the rule of Omri (c. 885-881-876 B.C.E.) and his successors in the northern kingdom, who practiced a policy of reconciliation and alliance with their neighbors. The peace with the southern kingdom was sealed by the marriage of the daughter of Omri's son and successor, Ahab (c. 876-853 B.C.E.), with the son of the southern king Jehoshaphat (c. 871-846 B.C.E. [see 2 Kings 8:18-26]). According to the Kurkh Monolith, a victory stela laid by the Assyrian king Shalmaneser III (c. 858-824 B.C.E.), "Ahab the Israelite" was part of a coalition including the Aramean kingdom of Damascus that fought against the Assyrians at the battle of Qarqar in 853 B.C.E. Ahab also sealed a peace with the Phoenician kingdom of Sidon by marrying Jezebel, daughter of King Ethbaal (1 Kings 16:31).

According to Assyrian texts, the Mesha Stela and the results of archaeological excavations at such sites as Hazor and Megiddo, the reigns of Omri and Ahab (874-853 B.C.E.) were marked by economic and political prosperity. The Bible, on the other hand, gives an entirely negative judgment: "Ahab son of Omri did evil in the sight of YHWH more than all who were before him" (1 Kings 16:30). How do we explain this contradiction?

The Omride Dynasty's economic and political success indirectly posed a serious religious problem: the diffusion of Baal worship among the Israelite population.[1] According to the Bible, Ahab

took as his wife Jezebel daughter of King Ethbaal of the Sidonians, and went and served Baal, and worshiped him. He erected an altar for Baal in the house of Baal, which he built in Samaria. Ahab also made a sacred tree [asherah] (1 Kings 16:31-33).

Later, King Jehu (c. 842-814 B.C.E.) ordered his men to burn the "stela of Baal" and destroy the Baal temple, which they converted into a latrine (2 Kings 10:26-27). This Baal temple in Samaria clearly had the three elements of the traditional sanctuaries: altar, stela and sacred tree.

Moreover this Samarian temple of Baal seems to have been served by a large staff: some 450 "prophets of Baal" (1 Kings 18:19). King Jehu later refers to "all the prophets of Baal," "all his worshipers" and "all his priests" (2 Kings 10:19). The Bible notes that the staff serving the Baal cult was maintained by Jezebel herself (1 Kings 18:19). Josephus recounts that the father of Ittobaal (biblical Ethbaal, father of Jezebel) seized the throne of Tyre after having been "a priest of Ashtarte."[2]

According to the customs of the time, a foreign royal wife, especially the daughter of king, was entitled to certain freedoms withheld from the local inhabitants. Solomon himself built sanctuaries for foreign gods out of respect for princesses or visiting diplomats. It would have been normal for Jezebel's husband to respect, and even facilitate, the practice of her personal religion by building a sanctuary where she could worship. This does not mean that Ahab repudiated his Israelite Yahwism; indeed, he gave the two sons who succeeded him as king, Ahaziah (c. 853-852 B.C.E.) and Jehoram (c. 852-841 B.C.E.), Yahwist names.

Nonetheless, this situation—with the Yahwist cult tolerant of a Baal cult in its midst—could easily result in conflict. As Phoenicians, Jezebel and the staff she maintained would have been respected as representing a people that was prosperous, technically sophisticated and culturally rich. There would have been a natural tendency to follow their ways, the ways of the Baal cult. Moreover, the Yahwism of this part of Israel, especially in the plains of Jezreel and Sharon and throughout Galilee, was probably rather superficial; the new Baal worship would have constituted a revival of ancient local Canaanite traditions. Ostraca (inscribed potsherds) from Samara, dating around the first quarter of the eighth century B.C.E., contain about as many "Baalist" names[3] as "Yahwist" names,[4] especially among farmers, which seems to indicate that Baalism was not limited to Phoenician foreigners or the immediate entourage of Jezebel.

According to the Bible, a powerful personality from Gilead, in the Transjordan, arose to confront the Baalist movement: the prophet Elijah the Tishbite (1 Kings 17:1ff.). The so-called Elijah cycle of the books of Kings (1 Kings 17:1 to 2 Kings 2:18) may well have been transmitted by Elijah's disciple, Elisha; these stories about Elijah were probably written down in Samaria during the reign of King Jehoash (c. 805-790 B.C.E.).[5]

Two episodes in the Elijah cycle are especially significant for the evolution of Yahwism: Elijah's confrontation with the prophets of Baal on Mount Carmel, and his pilgrimage to Horeb. In the first episode (1 Kings 18:18-46), Ahab agrees to Elijah's request to assemble the Israelites and the 450 Baal prophets on Mount Carmel, where Elijah challenges the Israelites: "How long will you go limping with two different opinions? If YHWH is God, then follow him; but if Baal, then follow him" (1 Kings 18:21). When no one answers, Elijah devises a test: Two bulls are to be chosen, as burnt offerings to Baal and YHWH. The bulls are to be prepared for sacrifice and placed on the altar, but the sacrifices are not to be lit. Instead, the Baal prophets are to pray to have Baal start the fire, and Elijah will pray to have Yahweh start the fire. The people will follow whichever god wins. The Baalists then prepare a bull for sacrifice, waiting in vain for the arrival of fire. Elijah repairs a Yahwist altar, prepares a bull for sacrifice on the altar, and prays to YHWH to set the offering ablaze—which he does, and the Israelites prostrate themselves, saying "YHWH indeed is the God."

Elijah's contest is a new departure, different from David's successful policy of reconciliation in which the Yahwist cult would absorb the features of the foreign ancestral god. Whereas YHWH could be assimilated to El, possibly as an avatar of El or as the supreme god of a pantheon that included El, this does not seem to be possible for Baal. It may be that YHWH and Baal were simply too much alike. Indeed, as we know from this episode and other biblical references, YHWH and Baal are both "gods of the storm," controlling the rains and thus maintaining the fruitfulness of the country.

Moreover, the story in 1 Kings 18:18-46 suggests that the Baalist party was on the rise while the Yahwists were in decline. That seems indicated not only by the number of prophets serving each deity—Baal: 450; Yahweh: 2 (1 Kings 18:22)—but also by the reference to "the altar of YHWH that had been thrown down" (1 Kings 18:30).

The choice of the place of this confrontation is probably significant. During the First Temple period, Mount Carmel constituted the border between Israel and the Phoenician kingdom of Tyre that extended along the Akko plain (see 1 Kings 9:11-14).[6] In choosing Mount Carmel, Elijah seems to say that the Baalists should not cross the border to penetrate into Israel; they should remain at home, in the kingdom of Tyre, the domain of Baal.

Finally, the confession of faith of the Israelites—"YHWH indeed is the God"—is sometimes understood as a monotheist confession of faith and translated as "YHWH is the [only] God." But this interpretation does not comport with the precise context of this episode. This confession of faith must be interpreted in light of Elijah's prayer asking God to light the fire: "O YHWH, God of Abraham, Isaac, and Israel, let it be known this day that you are God in Israel" (1 Kings 18:36). The purpose of the contest is not to determine the true God of the universe but rather the true God of Israel. The answer conforms to assertions often found in biblical texts from this period: YHWH is the God of Israel. The contest between Yahweh and Baal on Mount Carmel leads to a renewed assertion of Israelite monolatry.

After King Ahab tells Jezebel about YHWH's great victory over Baal, Jezebel threatens to kill Elijah, who then flees south. Near Beersheba, in despair over his inability to convince the Israelites to forsake Baal forever, Elijah sits under a tree and asks God to take his life. An angel of YHWH appears, telling Elijah to make a pilgrimage of "forty days and forty nights to Horeb [Sinai] the mount of God." On reaching the cave of Horeb, Elijah says to God:

I have been very zealous for YHWH, the God of hosts; for the
Israelites have forsaken your covenant, thrown down your altars,
and killed your prophets with the sword. I alone am left, and
they are seeking my life, to take it away (1 Kings 19:14).

YHWH responds by sending Elijah on a mission to recruit the king of Damascus (Hazael), the king of Israel (Jehu) and Elijah's successor (Elisha) to uproot and banish the Baalists (1 Kings 19:1-18).

Along with its mystical significance,[7] this episode helps illustrate some aspects of early Yahwism. First, as many biblical commentators have observed, Elijah's pilgrimage to Horeb, the "mount of God," makes him a kind of Moses, which in turn suggests that the Mosaic tradition was still alive in the second quarter of the ninth century B.C.E. (The reference to the Mosaic tradition is also made obvious in the role of "the cave," which is reminiscent of the "hollow of the rock" [Exodus 33:22] where YHWH appears to Moses.) Unfortunately, the text does not specify the nature of the connection between Elijah's visit to the mountain and Mosaic tradition. Nor are we told explicitly whether that tradition had been written down. Because Elijah's ninth-century B.C.E. pilgrimage was some 400 years later than Moses' 13th-century B.C.E. sojourn among the Midianites, the existence of some written source is likely.

Apparently, in confronting a severe crisis of Israelite Yahwism, Elijah felt it necessary to make a pilgrimage to the sources of Yahwism—which, as indicated by the early poems quoted in the first chapter, originated in the southern desert zone, outside the kingdoms of Israel and Judah. Elijah seems to have had no trouble finding the exact site of "Horeb the mount of God"; the "forty days and forty nights" probably simply means "a significant distance south of Beersheba." In any event, the fact that "Horeb the mountain of God" had a very specific (southern) locale did not pose any problem at the time.

Elijah's journey to Horeb is different from Moses' in one significant respect: In the Moses stories, the Midianite Yahwists, led by their priest, Moses' father-in-law Jethro, seem to be prospering. When Elijah arrives at Horeb, however, the sacred mountain seems abandoned and deserted. Indeed, we have seen that the Midianites disappeared from the historical record towards the beginning of the tenth century B.C.E., meaning that "Horeb the mount of God" had probably been abandoned for about a century. This pilgrimage to the sources of Yahwism revealed to Elijah that the situation of Yahwism was no better in its country of origin, Midian, than in Israel itself, where the Israelites had destroyed the YHWH altars.

This is the last time Horeb/Sinai appears in the Bible as an actual place, that is, as a place visited by a biblical figure; henceforth, it is a place to be evoked only in song and prayer. The future of Yahwism will not be played out at Horeb but in Israel itself. That is the meaning of Elijah's mission to join forces with Hazael of Damascus and Jehu of Israel, work that will be carried on by Elijah's disciple, Elisha.

The open crisis between Baalism and Yahwism in Israel will be finally settled, in theory at least, by the bloody coup of King Jehu (c. 841-814 B.C.E.), who "wiped out Baal from Israel" (2 Kings 10:28). This is followed a few years later by the destruction of a Baal temple that had been built in Jerusalem (2 Kings 11:4-18). To judge from the personal names on the many inscriptions (mostly seal impressions) from Judah of the eighth and seventh centuries B.C.E., Baal no longer had much influence in the southern kingdom.

Is this to say that polytheism, with YHWH coexisting among a number of Canaanite deities, was totally abandoned? A number of modern commentators think not, with some arguing that Israelite religion of the First Temple period was clearly polytheistic,[8] and that YHWH had an official consort.[9] We must therefore examine this historical question.

CHAPTER 7
"YHWH and His Asherah": Did the God of Israel Have a Consort?

About 30 years ago, I proposed that three lines of text inscribed in a tomb at Khirbet el-Qom, about 8 miles west of Hebron, consisted of a blessing formula reading, "by YHWH and his asherah."[1] Other similar blessing formulas have appeared about the same time among the paleo-Hebrew inscriptions of Kuntillet ʿAjrud, in the Sinai.[2] These epigraphic discoveries have altered the contexts in which we have come to understand the word *asherah* in the Hebrew Bible and have been the subject of numerous books. As one scholar has written, "Asherah studies are becoming, in their own right, a subset of ancient Near Eastern studies."[3]

The majority of these publications have tried to show that Asherah is the name of an official wife/consort of YHWH.[4] If we are to understand Israelite Yahwism of the First Temple period, then we must look in detail at this complex issue.

The 14th-century B.C.E. Amarna Letters often mention the name ʿAbdi-Ashirta ("Servant of Ashirta"), borne apparently by an Amorite king who was an enemy of the king of Byblos and who proclaimed himself a vassal of Egypt.[5] The divine name "Ashirta" is attested (as Ashratu) in Mesopotamian inscriptions from the reign of Hammurabi (c. 1792-1750) to the turn of the era more than 17 centuries later. Ashirta is the consort of the god Amurru and possibly carries the title "Lady of the steppe." The question arises as to whether Ashirta has re-emerged as biblical Asherah and as a consort of YHWH.

In the Amarna Letters, Ashirta appears only in the proper name 'Abdi-Ashirta. She is obviously related to the goddess Athirat, however, who is well attested in the neighboring kingdom of Ugarit. Excavations at Ugarit have brought to light nearly 2,000 tablets written in an alphabetical cuneiform script generally dating from the 13th century B.C.E.[6] and used until the destruction of the city in the early 12th century B.C.E.[7] The name of the goddess Athirat appears at least 74 times in these Ugaritic texts, including 55 times in myths or legends, 17 times in rituals,[8] once in correspondence and once in a fragment difficult to classify.[9] She is "the Lady Athirat of the sea (*rbt.aṯrt.ym*)," and has a sanctuary in Tyre (*qdš.aṯrt.ṣrm*); she is "procreatress of the gods (*qnyt.ilm*)." Although she is never called the wife of the great god Ilu/El, scholars have almost universally recognized her as his consort,[10] who assumed the role of the queen mother and placed her sons on the throne.

Curiously, the deity Athirat seems to disappear from Northwest Semitic texts in the first millennium B.C.E., at least in Phoenician and Aramaic texts. Indeed, in Phoenician and Aramaic, '*šrt* (athirat) is simply a common noun indicating a "sanctuary,"[11] and "Athirat" no longer appears as a separate divine name or as a theophoric element in personal names. The discovery of *l'šrt* on an earthenware jar in a sanctuary at Tell Miqneh/Ekron has prompted the excavators to interpret it as a reference to the goddess Athirat,[12] but this Philistine, or rather Philistian, inscription probably means only that the earthenware jar belongs "to the sanctuary."[13]

The only first-millennium B.C.E. references to the goddess Athirat appear in South Arabic epigraphy. According to the French scholar François Bron,

> The worship of Athirat in pre-Islamic South Arabia seems characteristic of the kingdom of Qataban, where she had a significant

sanctuary in Wadi Harib. She is attested in a more sporadic way at the site of as-Sawda. In Qataban, an object called *bḥt* was dedicated to her; if this term indicated truly a "votive phallus," as has been proposed, one would have a convincing indication that it was a fertility worship, but this translation remains hypothetical.[14]

It is in the context of the "disappearance" of the goddess Athirat in the first millennium B.C.E. that it is necessary to understand the problem arising from the term "asherah" in paleo-Hebrew epigraphy and in the Bible.

As we saw at the beginning of this chapter, the term "asherah" is mentioned in a mid-eighth century B.C.E. inscription from a tomb at Khirbet el-Qom, probably corresponding to biblical Makkedah (see, for example, Joshua 10:28).[15] The inscription is very difficult to read because it was incised twice, with the second incision only imperfectly covering the first one. After the publication of the site by the the excavator, William G. Dever,[16] I proposed a more complete reading of the inscription:[17] "Blessed be Uriyahu by YHWH and his asherah [*brk .'ryhw.lyhwh.w<l'šrth>*]." With some nuances about the order of the words, this reading has been accepted by most scholars.[18]

Excavations at Kuntillet 'Ajrud—a kind of caravansary in the northeastern Sinai during the first half of the eighth century B.C.E.[19]—brought to light several inscriptions written in ink on pithoi (in Hebrew script) and on the plaster surface of a wall (in Phoenician script). Some of these inscriptions are blessings similar to the one from Kirbet el-Qom: "I bless you by YHWH of Samaria and by his asherah (*brkt.'tkm.lyhwh.šmrn.wl'šrth*)" (pithos inscription); "I bless you by YHWH of Teman and by his asherah [*brktk lyhwh tmn wl'šrth*]" (pithos inscription); "by YHWH of Teman and his asherah [*l[y]hwh [?]tymn.wl'šrt[h]*]" (wall inscription); and "YHWH of Te[man and his asherah] made good to you [*hyṭb.yhwh.hty[mn.w'šrth]*]" (wall inscription).[20]

These attestations have often been interpreted as decisive evidence of the goddess Asherah, consort of YHWH.[21] However, the long list of contemporaneous Hebrew personal names does not include any theonym "Asherah," not even among the names from Khirbet el-Qom or Kuntillet 'Ajrud.[22] Moreover, "Asherah" is written *l'šrth,* with the grammatical suffix (*-h*) of the third person singular; such a construction is found nowhere else for a Hebrew proper name, not in the Bible or in the epigraphical record.[23] Finally, in the following sentence of the pithos inscription the verb *ybrk,* and in the wall inscription the verb *hyṭb,* are singular instead of plural as would be expected if two deities were mentioned. Given these facts, would it not be better to interpret "asherah" as a common noun?

In fact, according to a very old exegetical tradition attested by the Septuagint (a Greek translation of the Hebrew Bible, dating to the third and second century B.C.E.), Aramaic Targums and rabbinical exegesis, the common Hebrew noun *asherah* generally designates the sacred tree or thicket of a traditional sanctuary.[24] This interpretation clearly seems to correspond to most uses of *asherah* in the Hebrew Bible. Indeed, the context of *asherah* indicates that it is something that is wooden (Deuteronomy 16:21; Judges 6:25-30), that one plants (Deuteronomy 16:21),[25] that one tears off (Micah 5:14),[26] that one cuts (Exodus 34:13; Judges 6:25-30; 2 Kings 18:4, 23:14),[27] that one cuts down (Deuteronomy 7:5; 2 Chronicles 14:2, 31:1),[28] that one breaks down into parts (2 Chronicles 34:7, 34:4)[29] or that one burns (Deuteronomy 12:3; 2 Kings 23:15; 2 Chronicles 19:3).[30] It is also something that is often standing up (2 Kings 13:6; 2 Chronicles 33:19; Isaiah 27:9)[31] near the altar of YHWH (Deuteronomy 16:21-22).[32]

Consequently, the *asherah* is associated with YHWH in blessing formulas because this sacred tree placed in YHWH sanctuaries has assumed some of the sacred power of YHWH, especially his power of fertility. As shown by various Aramaic,[33] Hebrew,[34] Nabatean[35] and Greek[36] parallels towards the turn of the era, a sanctuary precinct or an object of worship can acquire the numinous power of the deity sufficiently to become associated with the deity itself, and it sometimes becomes a new divine name or even a new deity.

This interpretation of *asherah* as a common noun meaning "sacred tree" is clearly correct for the biblical references to *asherahs* in Yahwist sanctuaries, even when the practice of placing an *asherah* in a sanctuary comes under attack during the reforms of kings Hezekiah and Josiah (Deuteronomy 16:21-22).

Some scholars claim, however, that occasional references to *asherah* in the Bible should be interpreted as references to a consort of Baal. In Judges 3:7, for instance, we learn that the "Israelites did what was evil in the sight of YHWH, forgetting YHWH their God and worshiping the Baals and the Asherahs." And 1 Kings 18:19 mentions "four hundred prophets of *the* Asherah." The use of the definite article in this latter case and the plural form in the first suggests that both are common nouns, rather than proper names. Moreover, these passages are obviously late, written down around the time of Josiah's reforms (late seventh century B.C.E.) or later; to make the practice of setting up *asherahs* in Yahwist sanctuaries seem especially bad, the writers of the Deuteronomistic tradition simply associated it with Baal worship.

COURTESY WILLIAM DEVER

THIS ENIGMATIC DRAWING was found on the wall of an eighth-century B.C.E. tomb at Khirbet el-Kom, near Hebron; an accompanying inscription reads, "Blessed ... by Yahweh ... and his asherah." A similar inscription appears on an eighth-century B.C.E. sherd from Kuntillet ʿAjrud, in Sinai. Whether asherah referred to Yahweh's consort or simply to a sacred tree in temples to Yahweh is a matter of continuing debate among scholars.

Other references to *asherah* that are thought to refer to a goddess should probably instead be interpreted as referring to the sacred tree. The "carved image" of the asherah mentioned in 2 Kings 21:7 might simply refer to a representation of a sacred tree, an iconographic motif well known in the ancient Near East. The reference in 2 Kings 23:7 to a woman doing weaving for the asherah might refer to colored cloth placed on a sacred tree, a practice attested in Palestine as late as the 19th century.[37] In the Bible there is simply no definite reference to a goddess named Asherah.[38]

If no ancient Hebrew text unequivocally mentions a goddess named

Asherah, some archaeologists have suggested that she is represented by various objects or iconographic motifs, such as the sacred tree. Some argue that Asherah is more directly represented during the First Temple period (especially the eighth and seventh centuries B.C.E.) by the numerous female terracotta figurines that have been found in excavations of Judahite sites.[39] The argument that Asherah is depicted in these abundant terracotta figurines is very popular among scholars,[40] despite the fact that the statues do not present any characteristic features of deities. The terracotta statues may well be toys, or depictions of ordinary women, or votives of pregnant women hoping to induce abundant lactation (they have large breasts), and in the 1980s they were often identified as "Astarte" figurines. The only argument advanced in favor of the identification of the figurines with Asherah is her so-called "dominant position in the Old Testament" and the Khirbet el-Qom and Kuntillet-'Ajrud inscriptions.[41] We have just seen that this argument has little, if any, scholarly support. YHWH did not have a consort.

If the goddess Asherah was represented by the sacred tree, then she would have been the only great goddess surviving in eighth- and seventh-century B.C.E. Palestine.[42] This is not very likely. Moreover, the various proposals for an iconographic identification of the goddess Asherah in first-millennium B.C.E. are all completely hypothetical or based on circular reasoning.[43] Although we have solid references to the goddess Asherah in late-second-millennium B.C.E. Ugarit, there is not a single certain reference to her from first-millennium B.C.E. in Israel. Even if she did exist and was depicted, we have no knowledge whatever of the iconography.

In short, there is no reason to believe that First Temple period Yahwists believed YHWH had a consort named "Asherah." There is no indication that such a goddess was worshiped in Judah or Israel. However, an examination of the references to *asherah* reveals the importance of the sacred tree in traditional Israelite Yahwism and in the blessing formulas. The role of the *asherah*/sacred tree will in turn shed light on the religious reform of the Judahite king Hezekiah. First, however, it is necessary to delineate the aniconic character of Yahwism.

CHAPTER 8
Yahwism and Aniconism

How did people represent YHWH? Were there statues or representations of the God of Israel? The Second Commandment of the Decalogue seems to provide a clear answer:

> You shall not make for yourself an idol, whether in the form of anything that is in heaven above, or that is on the earth below, or that is in the water under the earth. You shall not bow down to them or worship them (Exodus 20:4-5; Deuteronomy 5:7-9).

This rather long commandment is probably the result of numerous editorial elaborations. The most primitive form may have been something like, "You will not make of me a carved representation [*pesel*]."[1]

The Bible never refers to any statue or anthropomorphic representation of YHWH. In the detailed description of the temple built by Solomon, probably according to a Canaanite-Phoenician model, there is no mention of a statue of the deity that one would normally expect to be placed in the holiest part of the sanctuary (1 Kings 6:16-28).[2] None of the many archaeological excavations of Israelite and Judahite sites has brought to light any carved image of the national divinity. This is very different from what we find in Mesopotamia and Egypt, where thousands of representations of deities have been unearthed. Although the Mesha Stela describes the Moabite king's conquest of YHWH sanctuaries of Atarot and Neboh, it makes no mention of any YHWH statue. The Bible gives a fairly detailed list of what the Babylonians carried off from the Jerusalem Temple, which they destroyed in 587 B.C.E.:

> The bronze pillars that were in the house of YHWH, as well as the stands and the bronze sea that were in the house of YHWH, the Chaldeans broke in pieces, and carried the bronze to Babylon. They took away the pots, the shovels, the snuffers, the dishes for incense, and all the bronze vessels used in the Temple service, as well as the firepans and basins. What was made of gold the captain of the guard took away for the gold, and what was made of silver, for the silver. As for the two pillars, the one sea, and the stands, which Solomon had made for the house of YHWH, the bronze of all these vessels was beyond weighing. The height of the one pillar was eighteen cubits, and on it was a bronze capital; the height of the capital was three cubits; the latticework and pomegranates, all of bronze, were on the capital all around. The second pillar had the same, with the latticework (2 Kings 25:13-17).

There is no reference to a statue or representation of the deity. Furthermore, while the Persian king Cyrus the Great returned statues of deities to other Near Eastern sanctuaries,[3] the Israelites received only "the vessels of the house of YHWH that [the Babylonian king] Nebuchadnezzar had carried away from Jerusalem and placed in the house of his gods" (Ezra 1:7).

Nonetheless, this Israelite religious aniconism has recently been questioned by some scholars.[4] These scholars rely on an inscription and some relief carvings of the Assyrian king Sargon II (c. 721-705 B.C.E.), who conquered the northern kingdom of Israel c. 722 B.C.E. A prism found at Nimrud, site of the ancient capital of Kalhu (biblical Calah),

(continued on page 73)

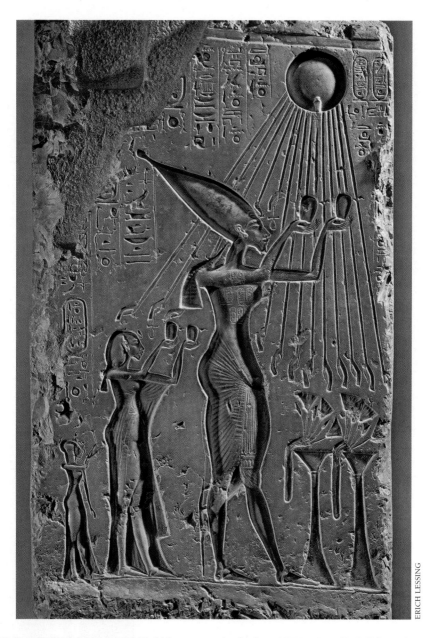

THE "HERETIC PHARAOH" Akhenaten (ruled c. 1359-1342 B.C.E.) and his famed wife Nefertiti worship Aten, represented by the sun disk at upper right. Akhenaten attempted to purge Egyptian religion of all gods except Aten and is often thought of as an early monotheist. A cache of some 300 cuneiform tablets found at Tell el-Amarna, Akhenaten's capital, provides an unparalleled window into the political, military and religious life of the ancient Near East.

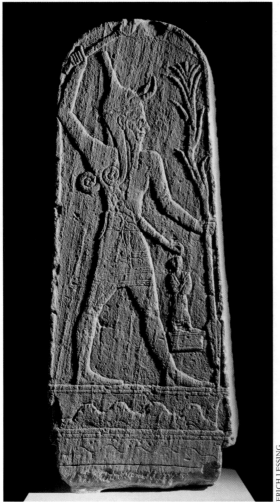

DEPICTED AS A MIGHTY WARRIOR, the Canaanite god Baal (top) brandishes a club in his right hand and a lance with branches representing lightning in his left. Baal attracted worshipers among the Israelites-and the ire of Israel's prophets.

The gold pendant at right depicts Astarte and emphasizes the goddess's sexual features. The figurine dates to the 16th-century B.C.E. and was found at Gezer. Astarte and her variant, Ashtoreth, were also popular among the Israelites and were condemned by the Biblical authors.

THE GODDESS HATHOR
displays her trademark
"flip" hairdo on an ivory
carving from Megiddo. An
important Egyptian deity,
Hathor was believed to
protect pregnant women
and mothers.

EL, CHIEF OF THE CANAANITE
PANTHEON, is shown seated
in this bronze statuette discovered at Megiddo. The figure is covered from head to
foot in gold foil and wears a
conical hat; its facial features
are highlighted by black inlay,
probably bitumen. "El" is a
generic name for God in
Northwest Semitic; in the
Hebrew Bible, God is often
called El.

THE CRAGGY CLIFFS OF EDOM reflect a reddish light, which gave the region its name (Edom means red). References in the earliest parts of the Bible suggest that Israelite religion was first formed in areas southeast and south of Israel, such as Edom and Midian.

THE TEL DAN STELA, from the second half of the ninth century B.C.E. was probably erected by King Hazael of Damascus to boast of a victory over Jehoram, king of Israel, and Ahaziah, king of Judah. It contains the first-known reference to King David outside the Bible-in the phrase "House of David" (high-lighted words at lower right). Ahaziah's Hebrew

name, Ahaziahu, contains at its end a form of YHWH, the personal name of the Israelite God.

MARYL LEVINE

"ISRAEL IS LAID WASTE" claims this stela carved by Pharaoh Merneptah (c. 1212-1202 B.C.E.). The name "Israel" appears in the highlighted area near the bottom of the stela and is shown in the detail. A hieroglyphic sign after the name indicates that "Israel" refers to a people-the earliest historical reference to the Israelites.

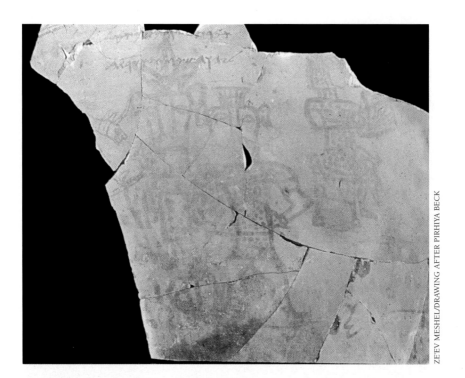

"I BLESS YOU BY YHWH of Samaria and by his asherah," reads the Hebrew inscription on this pithos, or storage jar, from Kuntillet 'Ajrud in the Sinai Desert. The illustration depicts two figures standing side-by-side with arms akimbo, a pose typical of the Egyptian god Bes. The larger one, at left, has a man's torso and posture, but a bovine face, horns and a tail. The smaller figure has a human body with breasts and a bovine face and tail. A seated musician appears at far right. Author André Lemaire disagrees with those scholars who identify the two standing figures as Yahweh and Asherah and suggest that Asherah was considered by some Israelites as Yahweh's consort.

70

FERTILITY FIGURINES such as these were common in ancient Judah. Many scholars believe they represent the goddess Asherah, though André Lemaire argues that they do not bear any distinctive signs of a deity and may simply be dolls or votives of pregnant women hoping to induce abundant lactation or eventually used as a kind of doll.

ASSYRIAN WARRIORS carry away ceremonial vessels as booty from the Judahite city of Lachish after their conquest in 701 B.C.E. The scene appears on the walls of the palace of Sennacherib in Nineveh but does not mean that there was a temple in Lachish or that King Hezekiah's reforms did not extend to Lachish.

ERICH LESSING

THE SYNAGOGUE at Gamla, atop a dramatic peak in the Golan Heights was in use from the late first century B.C.E. until its destruction by the Romans in 67 C.E. Synagogues, André Lamaire notes, functioned as both houses of study and of prayer. Ironically, they seem to have developed first in the Diaspora, then spread to Galilee and then last to Jerusalem.

DANNY SYON/GAMLA EXCAVATIONS/IAA

(continued from page 64)
and probably written towards the end of Sargon's reign, reports that the king took from Samaria as spoil "the gods in whom they entrusted." These "gods" have been connected to Assyrian reliefs representing the conquests of Sargon in which divine statues are taken as plunder from an unidentified city. Some scholars have identified the text *and* the images as representing the "gods of Samaria," which would imply not only that the Israelites created images of their gods but that Israelite religion was polytheistic.[5]

The weak points of this argument have been pointed out by Tel Aviv University historian Nadav Na'aman.[6] This Sargonic text was written down around 706 B.C.E., long after Sargon's conquest of Samaria in 722 B.C.E., and the sentence "and the gods in whom they entrusted I counted as spoils" is lacking in earlier copies of the text. The reference is thus apparently not a historical detail but a literary embellishment, like others in this text. The relief in question, moreover, does not show the capture of a Samarian city but of the Aramean city of Hamat in 720 B.C.E. On the other hand, a relief showing the Assyrian king Sennacherib's capture of Israelite Lachish in 701 B.C.E., well identified by a cuneiform legend, shows the plunder of cultic vessels but no statue representing the deity.

Even if the Assyrian evidence does not indicate that Yahwism was idolatrous, what about the "golden calves" installed at Dan and Bethel by the first ruler of the northern kingdom of Israel, Jeroboam I? After setting them up, Jeroboam even proclaims: "You have gone up to Jerusalem long enough. Here are your gods, O Israel, who brought you up out of the land of Egypt" (1 Kings 12:28). In fact, scholars have long considered this a polemical passage intended by the biblical author to discredit the worship in the temples of Dan and Bethel in favor of the Jerusalem Temple. In any event, in the ancient Near East the deity is often represented as standing on an animal that becomes the god's symbol. Thus Jeroboam's golden calves probably represented only "the support of the invisible presence of Yahweh, who in Jerusalem was sitting enthroned on the cherubim."[7] It is not a question of representing the divinity itself but of symbolizing its invisible presence in the temple by representing its support, and the expression "the one who sits on the

THE HOLY OF HOLIES at Arad's temple was flanked by two incense altars; against the back wall, placed on a stone base, was a standing stone with traces of red paint. André Lemaire believes this stone may have represented the deity. The Arad sanctuary was apparently used only briefly, from about 755 to 715 B.C.E., when it was destroyed, perhaps as part of King Hezekiah's religious reforms.

cherubim" (*yosheb [hak]kerubîm*) is probably borrowed from the iconography of the god El sitting on his royal throne.[8]

To understand Israelite aniconism, it is useful to look at the general context of aniconism in the ancient Near East. Following T.N.D. Mettinger,[9] we can distinguish between an "empty" aniconism, in which the presence of the deity is merely symbolized, and a "material" aniconism, in which the deity is represented, though not anthropomorphically. The Jerusalem Temple represents empty aniconism, for the presence of YHWH is symbolized by cherubim, which act as his throne; similarly, the YHWH sanctuaries in Dan and Bethel use a calf/bull to symbolize the presence of the deity. In material aniconism, on the other hand, the deity is directly represented, though not depicted. For example, excavators found a stone stela in the cella of a sanctuary at Arad; this stela likely signified the deity himself, not merely his throne. Both types of aniconism may have been characteristic of Yahwism.

We can also distinguish between "traditional" aniconism, which is simply passed from generation to generation, and "programmatic" aniconism, which is a clearly expressed policy that prohibits illustrated representations of the deity. The first may be tolerant and able to coexist comfortably with certain kinds of divine images; the second tends to exclude such representations systematically and may become iconoclastic.

In the ancient Near East, material aniconism was common. Aniconic stelae are attested from the third and second millennia B.C.E. in Syria—Mari,[10] Emar and Qatna—as well as in the southern Levant, especially in Gezer, Hartuv, Tel Kitan, Shechem, Megiddo and Hazor. During the first millennium B.C.E., according to the literary tradition, aniconic stelae were used in Gades, Paphos, Carmel and Emesa.[11] It also seems that the Nabateans were originally aniconic; the Nabatean use of anthropomorphic representations of divinities toward the end of the first millennium B.C.E. was probably due to the influence of Hellenism.[12]

Empty aniconism, on the other hand, is more difficult to detect archaeologically. Many scholars believe that some ancient depictions of sphinxes or cherubim, often carved in stone or ivory, may represent the thrones of deities. One in particular is dedicated by an inscription to Astarte, so the sphinxes/cherubim thought to represent empty aniconism are commonly called "Astarte thrones,"[13] even though they might have served as thrones for other deities as well. It is not certain, however, that these sphinx/cherub depictions were originally completely empty; the deity may simply be lost. Some reliefs may have representations. One relief also seems to show a standing stone (stela),[14] which might represent the convergence of the two types of aniconism.

Yahwistic aniconism appears to go back to its origins, to the Midianite cult practiced in the southern Negev. Archaeological surveys of the Negev and Sinai have revealed the existence of cult sites with standing stones as early as the 11th millennium B.C.E.[15] The Nabateans continued to practice material aniconism until about the turn of the era.[16]

In fact, material aniconism was practiced by most of Israel's neighbors. It seems to have been an intrinsic aspect of Canaanite civilization, in which it coexisted with forms of worship that were not aniconic and did make use of statues and other representations.

It is difficult to determine whether empty aniconism was equally common, though it does not seem to have been. Our evidence is largely limited to images of empty "thrones," especially from Phoenician-Canaanite culture, which apparently influenced the Temple of Solomon.

Thus traditional Yahwist aniconism was expressed in various forms, which leaves open the possibility that it underwent some kind of evolution. In the eighth and, especially, seventh centuries B.C.E., traditional Yahwism became increasingly programmatic—as kings Hezekiah and Josiah inaugurated reform movements inspired by the prophets, which purified Israelite aniconism.

CHAPTER 9

The Rise of the Prophets

I n the rejection of Baal worship, Elijah played a crucial role, as did his disciple and successor, Elisha. We call these men "prophets," those who proclaim the "word of YHWH." Prophecy has often been regarded as a unique feature of ancient Israelite society. According to the historian Ernest Renan, "The unique character of Israel starts with the prophets ... It is by prophecy that Israel occupies a special place in the history of the world."[1]

Since the publication of Assyrian and other Near Eastern texts beginning in the second half of the 19th century, however, it has been clear that Israelite prophecy was not an isolated phenomenon. The Mesha Stela, for instance, with two oracles of Chemosh (lines 14 and 32), was first published in 1870;[2] and an Assyrian cuneiform oracle was published in 1875.[3]

Taking into account only Semitic texts, and leaving aside the problem of Egyptian prophecy (which seems to have been common among senior officials), ancient Near Eastern prophecy is primarily attested in three groups of inscriptions: cuneiform texts from Mari on the Middle Euphrates (18th century B.C.E.), Assyrian oracles (seventh century B.C.E.) and Northwest Semitic inscriptions (ninth and eighth centuries B.C.E.).[4]

During the last half century the prophetic texts from Mari have been much studied, and excavations at the site continue to turn up new examples. We now have about 50 published texts that report oracles or symbolic gestures in letters generally intended for the king.[5] The king's servants were apparently obliged to tell the king directly about any divine oracles expressed by prophets. The majority of these oracles, it seems, were uttered during temple services; they were then immediately transcribed for the king, sometimes accompanied by the scribe's interpretation of the oracle. In this way, the king received a fresh and faithful account of the prophecy.

These prophetic oracles are generally introduced by the formula: "Thus speaks the god ..." According to the French scholar Dominique Charpin, "In the majority of cases, prophecies emanate from a deity who addresses the sovereign of the kingdom in which the temple stands."[6] The majority of these oracles have a nationalist tenor, affirming the deity's support for the king and promising the king victory over his enemies. Some prophecies are more complex, however, and some even have a certain "universalist" message, revealing the ambitions of such local divinities as Dagan of Terqa, Shamash of Andarig or Addu (=Hadad) of Aleppo. Addu is sometimes presented as a kind of World Master who dispenses justice:

Thus Addu speaks:
"I had given all the country to Yahdun-Lim
And, thanks to my weapons, he did not have any rival in
battle.
He gave up my party
And the country that I had given him, I gave it to Samsî-Addu
...
I put you back on the throne of your father ...
I anointed you with my victory oil
And no one stood in front of you.
Listen to this word from me:
When somebody who will have a lawsuit calls to you
By saying to you: 'Somebody made me wrong,'

Stand up and give him judgment;
Answer him righteously.
That is what I want from you.
When you depart for the battlefield,
Do not leave without hearing an oracle.
If the oracle that I give is favorable,
You will leave for the battlefield.
If it is not thus,
Do not cross the door!"[7]

The prophetic tradition of Mari is clearly similar to that attested in the Hebrew Bible.[8]

The same is true of Assyrian oracles of the seventh century B.C.E.[9] Assyrian prophets are especially designated by two terms: *mahhû* ("ecstatic") and *raggimu* ("the one who proclaims"), and they can be male or female. The oracles were proclaimed primarily during the reigns of Esarhaddon (c. 680-669 B.C.E.) and Assurbanipal (c. 668-631 B.C.E.). The god who most often speaks through the medium of the prophet is Ishtar of Arbela:[10]

Do not rely on man!
Raise your eyes and look at me!
I am Ishtar of Arbela.
I reconciled Assur with you.
When you were a child, I raised you towards me.
Do not fear anything, praise me.[11]

Certain tablets contain more than one oracle,[12] the first stage in the formation of a literary tradition of oracle collections.

Prophetic oracles are also attested in several West Semitic monumental inscriptions. The clearest example is that of the Aramaic stela of Zakkur, king of Hamat and Lu'ash (in Syria) at the beginning of the eighth century B.C.E. In the stela, Zakkur tells how, besieged in his capital, he turned to his principal god, Baal Shamayin (Master of Heaven), who answered him with oracles transmitted by *hâzîyîn* ("seers") and *'âdîdîn* ("spokesmen"):

And I raised my hands towards Baal Shamayin,
And Baal Shamayin answered me,
And Baal Shamayin (spoke) to me
Through seers and spokesmen
(And) Baal Shamayin (said to me):
"Do not fear!
Because it is I who made you king,
(And I, I) will stand with you
And I, I will deliver you from all (those kings who)
set up a siege against you."
And (Baal Shamayin) said to (me) ...
"All these kings who set up (against you a siege,
I will disperse them),
And this wall that (they built up,
I will cut down)."[13]

The late-ninth-century B.C.E. Mesha Stela does not specify the medium through which the oracles of the national divinity, Chemosh, were transmitted, but it quotes two oracles and tells how each one of them was later carried out:

And Chemosh said to me:
"Go, take Nebo from Israel."
And I went at night
And I fought there from break of dawn until midday.
And I took it and killed it whole:
Seven thousand men, boys, women, (girl)s and pregnant women,
Because I dedicated it to Ashtar-Chemosh.
And I took from there the altar-hear(ths) of YHWH
And dragged them in front of Chemosh ...
And the house of (Da)vid lived in Horonen ...?
And Chemosh said to me:
"Go down, fight against Horonen."
And I went down
And (I fought against the city

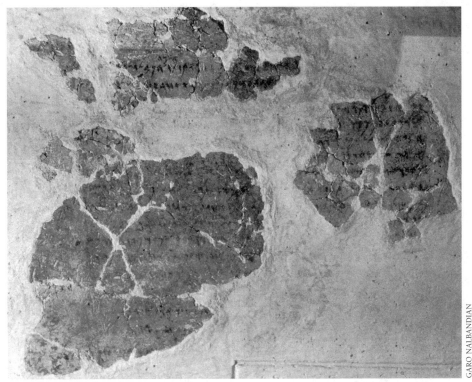

GARO NALBANDIAN

THE "BOOK OF (BA)LAAM (son of Be'o)r, the man who saw the gods," reads this inscription, in red and black ink, on the plaster wall at Deir 'Alla in the Jordan Valley. Balaam son of Be'or appears in Numbers 22-24, a foreign seer who prophesies in favor of Israel.

The inscription dates to the first half of the eighth century B.C.E. but likely reproduces a text that could go back to the ninth or tenth century B.C.E. This inscription shows that prophets were a part not only of Israelite religion but also of the religions of Israel's neighbors.

And I took it.
And) Chemosh (returned) it in my days.[14]

These two royal inscriptions not only reveal the existence of a prophetic tradition among contemporaneous kings in the vicinity of Israel, but also show that kings collected favorable oracles and inscribed them on monuments to propagate the royal ideology.

Another Aramaic inscription provides evidence of an old prophetic literature—an inscription in red and black ink on a plaster wall at Deir 'Alla in the middle Jordan Valley. According to the title, written with red ink, it is an extract of the "Book of (Ba)laam (son of Be'o)r, the man who saw the gods." The rest of the text, unfortunately badly preserved, reports that the gods revealed to Balaam an oracle of misfortune, which he, with sadness, conveyed to his people.[15]

According to paleographic analysis and the archaeological context, this inscription dates from the first half of the eighth century B.C.E., but it is obviously a copy of an earlier literary manuscript, on papyrus or leather, the composition of which could go back to the ninth or tenth century B.C.E. Such an Aramaic prophetic literature, apparently attached to the kingdom of Damascus, indicates the probable existence of a similar literature in the contemporaneous kingdoms of Israel and Judah. Moreover, the seer Balaam son of Be'or appears in the Bible; he is the principal character in Numbers 22-24, a foreign seer who prophesies in favor of Israel.

The existence of a prophetic tradition outside of Israel is thus attested in the Bible itself, as well as in the epigraphical record. Prophecy was not unique to Yahwism or to Israel; it was a more general religious phenomenon.

The fact that Israelite prophecy is not unique does not diminish the role of prophets in the development of Yahwism. The prophetic biblical texts clearly show that these "men of God" could play a very significant political and religious role. Some scholars have argued that the Israelite prophetic tradition was an invention of the Deuteronomistic History, which was re-edited during the Babylonian Exile. But the Deuteronomist probably simply developed an older historical tradition—with, perhaps, some exaggeration—by presenting a systematic account of earlier stories about prophecies and prophets.

The role of prophets in the history of Yahwism in the First Temple period is apparent from traditions reporting prophetic interventions by such prophets as Nathan (with respect to David and Solomon), Ahijah of Shiloh (Solomon and Jeroboam I), Elijah (Ahab) and Elisha (Jehoram, Jehu, Jehoahaz and Jehoash). This simple list suggests that transmitted oracles, announcing the fall of a king or his dynasty, could be used to legitimate the reign of that king's successor. In a way, then, oracles could become "king makers." Prophets were not only propagandists in service of the king, however, for they also denounced abuses of royal power (2 Samuel 12:1-15; 1 Kings 21) and fought the diffusion of Baal worship (1 Kings 18).

One important function of prophecy involved extending the influence of YHWH beyond the borders of Israel. For example, the fact that YHWH was the "God of Israel" (but not the god of territories beyond Israel), much as a king is the ruler of a kingdom (but not of territories beyond the borders of that kingdom), is suggested by David when he asks Saul why the king is pursuing him: "If it is YHWH who has stirred you up against me, may he accept an offering; but if it is mortals, may they be cursed before YHWH, for they have driven me out today from my share in the heritage of YHWH, saying, 'Go, serve other gods'" (1 Samuel 26:19).[16] Around 1000 B.C.E., then, to be exiled outside the territory of YHWH meant that one would have to serve other gods; YHWH apparently had no power outside Israel, and worship of YHWH stopped at Israel's borders.

But this was no longer true for the prophet Elijah, in the first half of the ninth century B.C.E. To escape Ahab and Jezebel, Elijah took flight out of Israel and even beyond neighboring countries that had extradition agreements with Israel (see 1 Kings 18:10). Thus he initially sought refuge near the Arabs of the country of Qedem (1 Kings 17:2-6);[17] then in Sarepta, in the kingdom of Sidon (1 Kings 17:8ff.); and finally on the mountain of God, in Horeb, beyond the kingdom of Judah (1 Kings 19:3-8).

The cycle of stories about the prophets Elijah and Elisha also tells of the extension of YHWH's power beyond the borders of Israel, especially into the Aramean kingdom of Damascus. The kingship of Hazael, for example, is in conformity with YHWH's plans (2 Kings 8:7-15; see 1 Kings 19:15).[18] Moreover, this cycle recounts the conversion of the Aramean general Naaman, who states, "there is no God in all the earth except in Israel" (2 Kings 5:15); Naaman recognizes only YHWH, even though he thinks of YHWH as literally attached to the territory of Israel and carries two mule-loads of Israeli earth (2 Kings 5:17).

The international character of YHWH's power becomes apparent in the oracles of later prophets, particularly Amos (mid-eighth century B.C.E.), who makes three general kinds of prophecy: (1) Oracles stating that nations will be punished for their transgressions against YHWH, not only Judah and Israel but most of the kingdoms of the southern Levant (Amos 1:3-2:3); (2) oracles stating that YHWH does not act simply in favor of the Israelites but is also the God of other nations, such as the Cushites, Philistines and Arameans (Amos 9:7); and (3) oracles suggesting that the misfortunes of other nations (Calneh, Hamath, Gath) will also strike Israel (Amos 6:2).

These three kinds of prophetic oracle are also characteristic of later prophets, particularly Isaiah, who prophesies the intervention of Egypt and Assyria (Isaiah 7:18-20; see also 5:26-30, 6:11-13, 8:7), with Assyria being simply an instrument in YHWH's hands (Isaiah 10:5ff.), and Jeremiah, who predicts the intervention of the Babylonian armies of Nebuchadnezzar (Jeremiah 5:15ff., 6:22ff., 13:20ff., 20:4ff.).

Even if some of these oracles developed late, the assertion of YHWH's power beyond the borders of Israel seems to go back to the prophets of the First Temple period. YHWH's actions are no longer limited to Israelite territory. Historically, this is not a new phenomenon; we have already seen, for instance, that the prophetic texts from 18th-century B.C.E. Mari tell of gods acting outside of their traditional territories.[19]

In a more general way, the tradition relating to Elijah reveals that prophets could pass down the prophetic tradition to disciples, or the "sons of prophets," who were associated with particular sanctuaries (Gilgal/Jericho, Bethel, Carmel). The Elijah cycle and Elisha cycle were probably composed toward the end of the ninth century B.C.E., even if they were not transmitted to us independently but were integrated into the historiographic tradition of the books of Kings.

Beginning in the eighth century B.C.E., the diffusion of writing led to the appearance of Hebrew prophetic books that remained independent of the royal historiographic tradition. Thus emerged the first "prophet-scribes": Amos and Hosea. The phenomenon of the prophet-scribe makes it possible to know more directly the thinking and teaching of the prophets themselves, rather than merely the consequences of their teaching for the king and his court.

We have seen that the earliest prophets tell of a more international Yahwism. We now will look at what the teachings of the prophet-scribes say about the Yahwism of the latter part of the First Temple period, the Exile, and the early Persian period, for these played a central role in transforming Israelite Yahwistic monolatry into a totally aniconic religion.

CHAPTER 10

The Religious Reforms of the Judahite King Hezekiah

Most of the prophecies of Amos of Tekoa (a town in Judah) seem to come from the reign of Jeroboam II of Israel (c. 790-750 B.C.E.), even though material was added later. These prophecies are thus contemporaneous with the Samaria ostraca and the Kuntillet ‘Ajrud and Khirbet el-Qom inscriptions, as well as with the copy of the book of Balaam inscribed on the plaster wall of Deir ‘Alla.

Although Amos is from Judah, he proclaims his oracles in the Bethel sanctuary in Israel (Amos 7:10ff.) and addresses peoples throughout the region: Damascus, Tyre, Philistia, Ammon, Moab, Edom, Judah and Israel. YHWH does not judge only the Israelites but also neighboring peoples; YHWH not only brought the Israelites out of Egypt but also the Philistines out of Caphtor and the Arameans out of Kir (Amos 9:7). Thus YHWH takes on the features of a great God with a regional domain who does not hesitate to criticize worship at the traditional Israelite high places (Amos 7:9) of Bethel, Gilgal and Beersheba.[1] Even the horns of the Bethel altar will be cut down (Amos 3:14).[2] Finally, YHWH prophesies the fall of Samaria and the deportation of Israelite leaders.

Soon after Amos comes Hosea to denounce the infidelity and the instability of the Israelites. Hosea is critical of the sanctuaries at Bethel (Hosea 12:3-5) and Gilgal, and explicitly denounces ritual practices in high places involving sacred trees (Hosea 4:12-15; see also 14:9 and Isaiah 1:29-30) and altars (Hosea 8:11, 12:12). Hosea reproaches the Israelites for making sacrifices to Baal and carved representations (Hosea 11:2, 13:1-2).

The prophecies of Micah (second half of the eighth century B.C.E.)[3] are set in a clearly monolatrous context: "For all the peoples walk, each in the name of its god, but we will walk in the name of YHWH our God forever and ever" (Micah 4:5). Nonetheless, Micah is also sharply critical of the traditional sanctuaries:

I will cut off sorceries from your hand,
and you shall have no more soothsayers;
and I will cut off your images and your stelae from among
you,
and you shall bow down no more to the work of your hands;
and I will uproot your sacred trees [asherim] from among you.
(Micah 5:13-14)[4]

Such prophecies imply a religious movement that protests abuses occurring in the traditional sanctuaries. According to 2 Kings, King Hezekiah (c. 727-699 B.C.E.) acted as a representative of this prophetic movement by carrying out a radical reform of the traditional sanctuaries:

He removed the high places, broke down the stelae, and cut down the sacred tree [asherah]. He broke in pieces the bronze serpent that Moses had made, for until those days the people of Israel had made offerings to it; it was called Nehushtan (2 Kings 18:4).

A little further on, 2 Kings recounts a speech by the Assyrian ambassador, who tries to convince the Jerusalemites to capitulate to the Assyrian army. In the course of his speech, he refers to the reforms of Hezekiah:

If you say to me, "We rely on YHWH our God," is it not he
whose high places and altars Hezekiah has removed, saying to
Judah and Jerusalem, "You shall worship before this altar in
Jerusalem"? (2 Kings 18:22).

Some scholars have questioned the historicity of Hezekiah's reforms.[5]
(We leave aside the question of whether the complementary accounts in
Kings and Chronicles used different sources.)[6] The historicity of the
reform described very briefly in 2 Kings 18:4 was probably based on an
early edition of Kings during Hezekiah's reign.[7] This composition is
characterized by its insistence that former kings of Judah "did not sup-
press [*lo'-sārū*] the high places [*habbāmôt*]," but Hezekiah was the one
who "removed/suppressed the high places [*hū' hésîr 'et-habbāmôt*]." This
was the essential aspect of the religious reform of Hezekiah (the sup-
pression of the high places), who insisted that previous kings be judged
according to their attitude toward the high places.

Hezekiah's reform appears to have been very daring, even revolution-
ary, striking at some of the main features of earlier Yahwism.[8] The elimination of Nehushtan, the famous bronze snake fashioned by Moses
according to Numbers 21:6-9,[9] suggests that Hezekiah did not hesitate
to criticize even aspects of the sacred Mosaic tradition. He also attacked
traditional sanctuaries that were attached by foundation legends to the
patriarchs. The Beersheba sanctuary with its altar and sacred tree, for
example, was associated with Abraham (Genesis 21:33) and Isaac (Genesis 26:25). Legends associated with the various patriarchs had legit-
imized the sacred stelae, trees and altars of the traditional sanctuaries.
They were now to be abolished.

Perhaps these measures had the support of refugees from the northern kingdom, which had been conquered by the Assyrians in 722 B.C.E.
The Samarians who settled in Judah—many in Jerusalem itself—would
not have been attached to traditional Judahite sanctuaries. Hezekiah
may also have had the support of his people in reaffirming the independence of Judah under the threat of an aggressive Assyrian empire.
Nonetheless, his reforms would have seriously upset the religious traditions of the provincial Judahite population, and they were probably not

easily accepted by the population as a whole.

Archaeological evidence from two sanctuaries in the Negev—Beer-sheba and Arad—suggests that at least some of Hezekiah's reforms were put into effect.[10] Although excavators at Beersheba have not found a sanctuary, they have uncovered a large stone altar with horns that had been re-used to build a wall apparently destroyed during the Assyrian king Sennacherib's campaign of 701 B.C.E.[11] This suggests that the altar had been torn down sometime earlier, very likely toward the beginning of Hezekiah's reign, when he undertook a building program to withstand a siege by the Assyrian army. Although the original site of this altar remains conjectural,[12] it seems clear that the altar itself was deliberately de-consecrated, for one of the horns was sawed off.

The stratigraphy of Arad, excavated by Israeli archaeologist Yohanan Aharoni between 1962 and 1967, remains in dispute. Another Israeli archaeologist, Zeev Herzog, has recently published a detailed report on Arad's Iron Age fortress, which contained a sanctuary excavated by Aharoni.[13] The sanctuary comprised a court with an altar for burnt offerings, an entry room (*hekal*) and a small holy of holies (*debir*) with an entrance marked by two incense altars. The holy of holies contained one stela (*massebah*) with traces of red paint, set up against the back wall. The Arad sanctuary was apparently in use only for a short period of time,[14] from about 755 to 715 B.C.E., when it was destroyed—probably as a result of Hezekiah's reforms.

Despite the archaeological evidence from Beersheba and Arad, which supports the biblical narrative, some archaeologists, such as Nadav Na'aman of Tel Aviv University, still believe that Hezekiah could not have carried out sweeping reforms in Judah. Na'aman argues that Assyrian reliefs depicting Sennacherib's capture of Judahite Lachish in 701 B.C.E. show bronze cult basins being carried off by Assyrian soldiers; according to him such cult basins imply that a sanctuary existed in Lachish at the time of its destruction,[15] which occurred after Hezekiah's reform. Also, in excavations at Lachish conducted between 1966 and 1968, Aharoni found the remains of a First Temple period sanctuary. Unfortunately, however, the stratigraphy of this sanctuary is not completely clear, and we do not know with any certainty when it was in

Z. RADOVAN/WWW.BIBLELANDPICTURES.COM

HORNS AT EACH CORNER were typical of Israelite altars. This one was part of a temple in Beersheba, though one of its horns was sawed off, probably as part of King Hezekiah's religious reforms that sought to centralize worship in Jerusalem. This altar was reassembled by archaeologists; it had been taken apart in ancient times and its stones reused in a wall destroyed by the Assyrian king Sennacherib in 701 B.C.E.

use.[16] In his final publication of the Lachish excavations,[17] David Ussishkin dates this sanctuary to the ninth-eighth century B.C.E. with a possible destruction during Hezekiah's reform or a little earlier c. 760 B.C.E.

As for the basins shown in the Assyrian reliefs, we do not know that they had any religious purpose. In fact, one of Na'aman's colleagues at Tel Aviv University, archaeologist David Ussishkin, specifically makes the argument that the vessels shown in the Assyrian reliefs were not cultic: "The second and third soldiers bear large ceremonial chalices. These resemble in general smaller Iron Age cultic vessels, but here they probably had a purely ceremonial function."[18]

There is thus little reason to doubt the biblical account concerning Hezekiah's reforms.[19] And they were radical reforms, cutting Yahwism from its traditional local, geographical and cultural roots. The Yahwism that began as worship of "the god of the father"—in that god's sanctuary, with that god's sacred tree (*asherah*) and standing stone—was drastically changed toward the end of the eighth century B.C.E., in four principal ways:

> First, the official center of worship was now in the Jerusalem Temple. Yahwism thus became less at risk of losing its fundamental unity. Indeed, the blessing formulas from Kuntillet 'Ajrud mentioning "YHWH of Samaria" and "YHWH of Teman" suggest that Yahwism was evolving very differently, toward a plurality of YHWHs, each with its own sanctuary and features, little by little obliterating whatever it was that held each of these YHWHs together in a single divine personality. Something similar is found with cults of the Virgin Mary in Catholic tradition; in popular religion, "Our Lady of Chartres," "Our Lady of Lourdes" and "Our Lady of Fatima" tend to become different personalities.[20]

The sharp prophetic criticism of the various sanctuaries is directed at this evolution in popular religion towards a plurality of local YHWHs.[21] It is clearly formulated by the Deuteronomist:[22]

> You must demolish completely all the places where the nations whom you are about to dispossess served their gods, on the mountain heights, on the hills, and under every leafy tree. Break down their altars, smash their stelae, burn their sacred trees [*asherim*] with fire, and hew down the idols of their gods, and thus blot out their name from their places. You shall not worship YHWH your God in such ways. But you shall seek the place that YHWH your God will choose out of all your tribes as his habitation to put his name there [*lāšūm 'et-šemô šām*] (Deuteronomy 12:2-5).[23]

It is also this opposition to the various local Yahwist sanctuaries that explains the Deuteronomist's insistence on the unity of the national deity: "YHWH our God, YHWH is one" (Deuteronomy 6:4).

Second, in the blessing formulas in the inscriptions from Kuntillet 'Ajrud and Khirbet el-Qom, the sacred tree seems to have acquired some of the numinous character of the deity, so as to become semi-divine. In popular religion, the stela and the altar (especially its horns) probably came to be regarded as so sacred as to become divine. Thus the eighth-century B.C.E. prophets protested against this evolution, calling for the destruction of sacred trees, stelae and altars. Once again, this reaction of the prophets is codified in Deuteronomy: "You shall not plant any tree as a sacred tree [asherah] beside the altar that you make for YHWH your God; nor shall you set up a stela [massebah]—things that YHWH your God hates" (Deuteronomy 16:21).

Third, the elimination of the sacred tree and the stela from Yahwist sanctuaries meant that Yahwism was consistent with only "empty aniconism," expressed in the architecture and furniture of the Jerusalem temple where the divine presence was symbolized by the empty throne of the cherubim. "Material aniconism," represented by the stela, was rejected and the deity was simply evoked by the vacuum. The aniconism of Yahwism thus reached a significant new stage, becoming programmatic and absolute.[24]

Last, the concentration of worship in Jerusalem emphasized the religious unity of the Israelites, especially by means of the institution of pilgrimage festivals held in Jerusalem (see Isaiah 2:2-3). The disappearance of the local sanctuaries implied the disappearance of specific local festivals held in association with those sanctuaries. Thus the three annual pilgrimage festivals in Jerusalem (Exodus 23:14-17, 34:18-23; Deuteronomy 16:1-16) became all the more important. Yahwist religion was becoming less and less rooted to a particular piece of earth, and more and more rooted in the conception of the "people of YHWH."

On the whole, then, Hezekiah's reforms represented a movement away from both the origins of Yahwism and from the Yahwism that was popularized by David. King David had promoted a policy of tolerance and integration; he sought to bring the various local sanctuaries and religious traditions together under the name of YHWH. Thus, YHWH could take root in sanctuaries throughout Israel. Hezekiah's reforms, on the other hand, constituted a geographical uprooting of provincial Yahwisms, centering them in Jerusalem as a single and regularized Yahwism.[25]

Despite his reforms, Hezekiah led Judah into political, military and economic disaster. The Assyrians, who had destroyed the northern kingdom in 722 B.C.E., also had designs on the south. If the Assyrian king Sennacherib (704-681 B.C.E.) was unable to take Jerusalem (which only added to Jerusalem's religious prestige), he nonetheless ravaged the Shephelah and Negev, killing thousands of people, taking numerous prisoners and forcing Hezekiah to pay a heavy tribute of "thirty gold talents" (2 Kings 18:14), a figure confirmed by the Assyrian annals of Sennacherib. For part of the population, this disaster was probably interpreted as a consequence of the drastic, even "impious," measures taken against the local sanctuaries (see 2 Kings 18:22,25). Hezekiah's religious reforms were quickly forgotten during the reign of his successor, Manasseh (c. 699-645 B.C.E.). Similar reforms, however, were to be advocated later in the seventh century B.C.E. by King Josiah (c. 640-609 B.C.E.).

Astral Worship and the Religious Reforms of King Josiah

The Second Book of Kings describes the return to early Yahwism under Hezekiah's successor, Manasseh:

For he [Manasseh] rebuilt the high places that his father Hezekiah had destroyed; he erected altars for Baal, made a sacred tree [asherah], as King Ahab of Israel had done, worshiped all the host of heaven, and served them ... He built altars for all the host of heaven in the two courts of the house of YHWH. He made his son pass through fire; he practiced soothsaying and augury, and dealt with mediums and wizards (2 Kings 21:3-6).

There is no doubt about the polemical character of this passage.[1] The authors of the Deuteronomistic History were determined to make Manasseh appear as evil as possible—probably so that Manasseh, not the "good" king Josiah, would appear ultimately responsible for the fall of Jerusalem to the Babylonians in 587 B.C.E.

This description is especially striking because of its reference to worship of the stars. Many of Manasseh's faults, such as worshiping "the host of heaven," are also attributed to the Israelites of the northern kingdom just before it was conquered by Assyria (2 Kings 17:16-17). Both passages, however, are part of the Deuteronomistic History composed during the reign of Josiah and then re-edited during the Babylonian captivity.[2]

Interestingly, the denunciation of star worship does not begin until the latter part of the seventh century B.C.E., with the prophecies of Jeremiah and Ezekiel:

> Do you not see what they are doing in the towns of Judah and in the streets of Jerusalem? The children gather wood, the fathers kindle fire, and the women knead dough, to make cakes [*kawwânîm*] for the queen of heaven (Jeremiah 7:18; see also 44:17-19).

> The bones of the kings of Judah, the bones of its officials, the bones of the priests, the bones of the prophets, and the bones of the inhabitants of Jerusalem shall be brought out of their tombs; and they shall be spread before the sun and the moon and all the host of heaven, which they have loved and served, which they have followed, and which they have inquired of and worshiped (Jeremiah 8:1-2).

> And the houses of Jerusalem and the houses of the kings of Judah shall be defiled like the place of Topheth—all the houses upon whose roofs offerings have been made to the whole host of heaven, and libations have been poured out to other gods (Jeremiah 19:13).

> He brought me to the inner court of the house of YHWH;[3] there, at the entrance of the temple of YHWH, between the porch and the altar, were about twenty-five men, with their backs to the temple of YHWH, and their faces toward the east, prostrating themselves to the sun toward the east (Ezekiel 8:16).

This astral worship is explicitly rejected by Deuteronomy:

When you look up to the heavens and see the sun, the moon, and the stars, all the host of heaven, do not be led astray and bow down to them and serve them (Deuteronomy 4:19).

If there is found among you, in one of your towns that YHWH your God is giving you, a man or a woman who does what is evil in the sight of YHWH your God, and transgresses his covenant by going to serve other gods and worshiping them, whether the sun or the moon or any of the host of heaven ... then you shall bring out to your gates that man or that woman who has committed this crime and you shall stone the man or woman to death (Deuteronomy 17:2-3,5).

Such star worship is not mentioned in the account of Hezekiah's reforms, so it probably took root in Jerusalem between the reign of Hezekiah and the fall of Jerusalem to the Babylonians in the early sixth century B.C.E.

According to Zephaniah 1:5, star worship was practiced especially in the Temple and on the terraces of houses. In the second half of the seventh century, star worship came under severe attack by King Josiah,[4] who "deposed the idolatrous priests whom the kings of Judah had ordained to make offerings in the high places at the cities of Judah and around Jerusalem; those also who made offerings to Baal, to the sun,[5] the moon, the constellations [mazzalôt] and all the host of the heavens" (2 Kings 23:5). "The altars on the roof of the upper chamber of Ahaz, which the kings of Judah had made, and the altars that Manasseh had made in the two courts in the house of YHWH, he [Josiah] pulled down from there and broke in pieces, and threw the rubble into the Wadi Kidron" (2 Kings 23:12).

The historical context of the development of star worship in Judah is clear: It developed during the period when the Assyrians and later the Babylonians dominated the Levant. That is, Israelite star worship was strongly influenced by Mesopotamian astral worship.[6] This Mesopotamian influence is apparent linguistically in the borrowing of two Akkadian words, kawwânîm for the cakes offered to the "queen of heaven" in Jeremiah 7:18 and 44:19,[7] and mazzalôt to indicate the "constellations" in 2

Kings 23:5.[9] The "queen of heaven" is therefore the great Mesopotamian goddess Ishtar, which seems confirmed by the iconography of some seals and jewelry from this time.[9]

Star worship was a significant phenomenon in Aramean culture and religion as well. The Aramean pantheon included the god of heaven Baal Shamayin, the sun-god Shamash, the moon-god Sahar,[10] and such constellations as the Pleiades. In fact, the Assyrian empire of the first half of the first millennium B.C.E.[11] was an Assyrian Aramean empire, and similar forms of star worship were practiced by both Assyrians and Arameans; we see this clearly in contemporaneous iconography,[12] particularly in seals and seal impressions.[13]

As we have seen, King Josiah attacked the Mesopotamian-influenced star worship with surprising violence. This violence may be explained by Josiah's ultimate intention of reaffirming the independence of the Judahite kingdom, especially as the Assyrian empire weakened and then collapsed under the onslaught of the Babylonians. The firm, official rejection of all forms of foreign worship,[14] which had even come to affect worship in the Jerusalem Temple, makes perfect sense in the context of such a "nationalist" movement.

Josiah's reform had some success.[15] For instance, numerous Yahwist names appear on Judahite ostraca, seals and seal impressions from the seventh and early sixth century B.C.E.,[16] as indicated by the recent publication of a group of West Semitic seals[17] and two volumes of bullae (seal impressions).[18] This phenomenon is best explained by a resurgence of monolatrous Yahwism in Judahite religion of that time.[19]

Josiah died in Megiddo in 609 B.C.E. His successors were confronted by a rivalry between Egypt and Babylonia (which had wrested supremacy from Assyria in Mesopotamia) for control of the Levant. The Babylonian king Nebuchadnezzar II first laid siege to Jerusalem in 597 B.C.E. A decade later, he set fire to the city, its royal palace and its temple, deporting part of its population to Babylonia. The country was transformed into a simple province managed by a Judahite puppet named Gedaliah; later, after Gedaliah's assassination as a "collaborator," the province was probably run by a Babylonian governor. Could Yahwism survive this decimation of the "people of YHWH"?

CHAPTER 12
The Religious Crisis of Exile

Until the Babylonian Exile, YHWH remained primarily the "God of Israel," the national deity of the Israelites who lived in the territories of Israel and Judah and worshiped at the Jerusalem Temple. After the Babylonians conquered Jerusalem and destroyed the Temple in 587 B.C.E., they resettled the Israelite political and religious elites in Babylonia; these exiled leaders included priests and such prophets as Ezekiel.

The Exile meant a deep and painful crisis for Yahwism. If the "god of the father" had become YHWH the "God of Israel," he nonetheless retained an essential connection to the land of his people. Originally, YHWH's sanctuary was at Horeb/Sinai, in the south and later in Shiloh in Cisjordan; then, after David, YHWH's sanctuaries were in the entire Land of Israel; and then, with the reforms of Hezekiah and Josiah, YHWH's sanctuary was exclusively the Jerusalem Temple, though he remained the God of all Israelites. Despite this evolution, YHWH was always firmly attached to a place; he was the God of his place, Israel and Judah, while other gods were sovereign in their places. Now, however, with the Exile, this monolatrous Yahwism had to change fundamentally or become extinct.

MARDUK was the patron deity of the city of Babylon and the chief god of the Babylonian pantheon. When the Israelites found themselves in exile in Babylonia after 587 B.C.E., they faced a theological crisis: The temple of their God, Yahweh, lay in ruins in Jerusalem, yet Marduk and other gods were worshiped in grand temples throughout Babylonia. Did that mean Marduk was mightier than Yahweh?

Yahwism could no longer be simply a religion practiced in Israel and Judah, with its official cult limited to the Jerusalem Temple. Not only was the Temple destroyed, but the Judahites were now forced to live under the jurisdiction of a different god—or, rather, gods, for the Babylonians were polytheists who worshiped multiple deities.

One factor in the survival of Yahwism was the Babylonian policy of resettling exiled peoples in their own communities. That is, exiled Phoenicians were resettled in Phoenician villages, and exiled Philistines were resettled in Philistine villages in Babylonia. From ancient cuneiform texts found at Babylon, we know of villages of deportees with such names as Ashkelon and Gaza (Philistine cities), as well as Tyre and Kedesh (Phoenician cities). These villages were a kind of New Ashkelon and New Tyre, much like our New York and New Orleans.

The exiled Israelites were also aggregated in their own communities.

The Book of Ezekiel, for example, describes just such a setting in which the prophet answers questions from the elders and other leaders gathered around him. Moreover, a recently published cuneiform tablet dating to 498 B.C.E.,[1] inscribed with names of deported Israelites, was composed at a place called "Al Yâhûdu" (meaning "the town of Judah"), which is the Babylonian Akkadian name for Jerusalem. This Al Yâhûdu, however, clearly refers to a village in Babylonia—a New Jerusalem, where people from the Judahite capital were resettled.

Living among the Babylonians, the exiled Judahites must have wondered: Did the Babylonians so completely overwhelm Judah because their gods were stronger than YHWH? Large temples of the Babylonian gods Marduk, Nabu and Ishtar, among others, graced Babylonian cities, reflecting the economic prosperity and power of the people who served these gods. The Temple of YHWH in Jerusalem, on the other hand, the only temple where YHWH could be worshiped following the reforms of Hezekiah and Josiah, lay in ruins. Under these conditions, with Israel and Judah completely overrun and with the Temple destroyed, what would it mean to serve YHWH as the "God of Israel"?

The Judahites in Babylonia, moreover, would have witnessed an atmosphere of rich religious ferment. Especially during the reign of the Babylonian empire's last king, Nabonidus (c. 556-539 B.C.E.), the various gods of Babylonia were in continual rivalry with one another, with their adherents making claims for their god's supremacy. The partisans of Marduk, for example, whose center of worship was Babylon, tried to outdo the partisans of the moon-god Sin, whose greatest temple had been rebuilt in Harran and who may have been supported by Nabonidus himself.[2] Akkadian texts from this time recount a kind of theological contest in which the followers of Marduk or Sin chant hymns saying that their god is incomparable, the most beautiful and the most powerful.

Given these conditions, the fact that Israelites were resettled in their own communities, along with their priests and prophets, allowed them to address the religious crisis in a more coherent way. Initially, under the reign of Nebuchadnezzar II (604-562 B.C.E.), the prophet Ezekiel explained to the Israelites that the catastrophe that had struck them was the result not of the impotence of YHWH but of the Israelites' repeated disregard of his commandments. Thus YHWH speaks through the agency of the prophet Ezekiel:

> I myself will bring a sword upon you, and I will destroy your high places. Your altars shall become desolate, and your incense stands shall be broken; and I will throw down your slain in front of your idols (Ezekiel 6:3-4).

> Soon now I will pour out my wrath upon you;
> I will spend my anger against you.
> I will judge you according to your ways,
> and punish you for all your abominations
> (Ezekiel 7:8).

Ezekiel's explanation for the Israelite catastrophe is not new. The late-ninth-century B.C.E. Mesha Stela (lines 5-6) attributes the oppression of Moab to the anger of the Moabite national deity, Chemosh: "Omri was king of Israel, and he oppressed Moab for many days, for Chemosh was angry with his land." In other words, such oppression is not inconsistent with the power of YHWH as the "God of Israel." Ezekiel apparently hoped for a revival of Yahwism led by those deported to Babylonia, because the divine presence had left Jerusalem (Ezekiel 1) to rest among the exiles in Babylonia, close to the river Chebar (Ezekiel 10:20-22). It is important to note, then, that Ezekiel's YHWH is not confined to his "sanctuary" in Israelite territory or Jerusalem. YHWH is in the midst of his people wherever they are.

The aniconism of Yahwism—especially the programmatic aniconism mandated by the reforms of Hezekiah and Josiah—also served the Judahites well in Babylonia. They would have been confronted on a daily basis with images of Mesopotamian gods, especially the divine statues in temples. Even though these images represented the gods of the powerful Babylonians who had conquered the Israelites and taken them into exile, the Israelites rejected the attraction of these deities, following Ezekiel's warning: "What is in your mind shall never happen—the thought, 'Let us be like the nations, like the tribes of the countries, and worship wood and stone'" (Ezekiel 20:32).

The prophets forcefully affirm that images of the gods are not gods but merely things made by men. For example, the anonymous prophet Deutero-Isaiah (Second Isaiah), who lived in Babylonia in the second half of the sixth century B.C.E. (chapters 40-55 of the Book of Isaiah are attributed to Deutero-Isaiah), writes that "Bel [Bel-Marduk, chief god of Babylon] bows down, Nebo [the son of Bel-Marduk] stoops, their idols are on beasts and cattle" (Isaiah 46:1). What is an "idol?" asks Deutero-Isaiah: "A workman casts it, and a goldsmith overlays it with gold, and casts for it silver chains" (Isaiah 40:19). Those who make idols do so in vain, he says:

ISHTAR, THE GODDESS OF LOVE stands astride a lion, a symbol closely associated with the Mesopotamian goddess. During the periods of Assyrian and Babylonian domination over ancient Israel (eighth-sixth centuries B.C.E.), Mesopotamian astral worship greatly influenced Israelite religion. The Bible condemns the practice of offering cakes to the "queen of heaven" (Jeremiah 7:18, 44:19), a reference to Ishtar.

All who make idols are nothing, and the things they delight in do not profit; their witnesses neither see nor know. And so they will be put to shame. Who would fashion a god or cast an image that can do no good? Look, all its devotees shall be put to shame; the artisans too are merely human (Isaiah 44:9-11).

This kind of derision expressed with regard to divine images appears in the Book of Jeremiah, too, though in a passage inserted into the text after the time of the prophet:

> Their idols are like scarecrows in a cucumber field,
> and they cannot speak;
> They have to be carried, for they cannot walk.
> Do not be afraid of them, for they cannot do evil,
> nor is it in them to do good.
> (Jeremiah 10:5)

The rejection of Babylonian-style idol worship, with its numerous divine statues and numerous rituals performed in honor of these images,[3] such as "washing the god's mouth [mîs pî],"[4] subsequently became a traditional aspect of prophetic preaching and literature.[5] When later redactors edited the Deuteronomistic History (which includes not only the book of Deuteronomy but also the books of Joshua, Judges, Samuel and Kings), they added the strong message that the making and worshiping of divine images violated YHWH's commandments. For example, Deuteronomy 4:27-28—"YHWH will scatter you among the peoples ... There you will serve other gods made by human hands, objects of wood and stone that neither see, nor hear, nor eat, nor smell"—was clearly inserted after the Babylonian captivity into the older text of Deuteronomy, which had been composed near the end of the seventh century B.C.E.

If the Babylonian gods were simply "objects of wood and stone" made by "human hands," what about YHWH?

CHAPTER 13

The Emergence of Universal Monotheism

T he religious ferment during Nabonidus's reign—with the great god Marduk vying with the great god Sin for pride of place in the Babylonian pantheon—forced the Israelites to ponder the role of YHWH outside of Israel. If YHWH had indeed followed his people into Babylonia, what was his relation to the Mesopotamian gods? If the Babylonian gods were just "objects of wood and stone," then was YHWH the only true God, acting not only in Babylonia but throughout the universe?

This understanding of YHWH as the universal God emerges in Deutero-Isaiah, written during the reign of the Persian king Cyrus the Great (559-530 B.C.E.), who conquered the Babylonians and replaced them as the Near Eastern superpower. The prophet quotes YHWH: "Before me no god was formed, nor shall there be any after me" (Isaiah 43:10); and "I am the first and I am the last; besides me there is no god" (Isaiah 44:6). It was YHWH, says Deutero-Isaiah, "who created the heavens (he is God!), who formed the earth and made it. He established it; he did not create it a chaos; he formed it to be inhabited!" (Isaiah 45:18).

In Deutero-Isaiah, YHWH's role as creator is a fundamental aspect of his universal power: "I made the earth, and created humankind upon it; it was my hands that stretched out the heavens" (Isaiah 45:12). The idea of YHWH as creator-god is not expressed for the first time in Deutero-Isaiah; YHWH's role as creator emerged early on as a result of his assimilation with *El Elyon* (God Most High). Nonetheless, it now becomes an essential feature of YHWH: He created the entire world and the entire world depends upon him.

Monotheism and universalism go hand in hand, and the prophet quotes YHWH as commanding the entire universe to recognize him as the one and only God: "I am YHWH, and there is no other; besides me there is no god ... [so let all the peoples] know, from the rising of the sun and from the West, that there is no one besides me" (Isaiah 45:5-6). Or this:

There is no other god besides me,
A righteous God and a Savior;
there is no one besides me.
Turn to me and be saved,
all the ends of the earth!
For I am God, and there is no other.
(Isaiah 45:21-22)

Here we have a full-blown monotheism. The prophet is not saying that YHWH is the greatest of all the gods but that YHWH is the only God. Nor is the prophet saying that YHWH is the god only of the people of Israel; he is the God of everyone everywhere. This is not monolatry in the grand old tradition of Yahwism, in which the "god of the father" became the "God of Israel." This is something completely new: YHWH is the universal God, "and there is no other."

In this spirit, as we have seen with respect to the severe strictures against divine images, biblical redactors re-edited and re-published the ancient texts to make them consistent with a strict monotheism. Thus they added monotheistic passages to Deuteronomy: "To you it was shown [that is, YHWH's power in leading the Israelites out of Egypt] so that you would acknowledge that YHWH is God; there is no other besides him" (Deuteronomy 4:35). "So acknowledge today and take to heart that YHWH is God in heaven above and on the earth beneath; there is no other" (Deuteronomy 4:39). Similar passages were also inserted elsewhere in the Deuteronomistic History; in Kings, for instance, King Solomon prays "that all of the peoples of the earth may know that YHWH is God; there is no other" (1 Kings 8:60).

This sudden emergence of Yahwist monotheism,[1] in a Mesopotamian context, is all the more astonishing in that we know almost nothing about the author of Deutero-Isaiah, the prophet who gave it such a clear expression. One of the few things we do know about him is that he was an admirer of the Persian empire and that he found favor with the greatest Persian king, Cyrus.[2] According to Deutero-Isaiah, it is YHWH himself

who says of Cyrus, "He is my shepherd,
and he shall carry out all my purpose;"
and who says of Jerusalem, "It shall be rebuilt,"
and of the temple, "Your foundation shall be laid."
Thus says YHWH to his anointed, to Cyrus,
whose right hand I have grasped
to subdue nations before him
(Isaiah 44:28-45:1).

Is it possible, then, that Deutero-Isaiah's strict monotheism influenced Persian religion—and/or Persian religion influenced Yahwism? Indeed, according to the early fifth-century B.C.E. Greek historian Herodotus, the Persians "do not erect statues of gods in their temples or altars, and they consider such people who do raise divine statues to be mad; the reason for this, in my opinion, is that, unlike the Greeks, the Persians never considered the gods as comparable in nature to men."[3] Persian religion thus seems to have shared an aniconism with Yahwist tradition. Moreover, the Persian god Ahuramazda was also a creator-god. A statue of the Persian king Darius I (c. 522-486 B.C.E.), found at Susa, is inscribed, "Ahuramazda is the great god who created the earth, who created the heavens, who created man."[4]

Unfortunately, we know little about Persian beliefs and religious practices at the time of Cyrus and his son and successor, Cambyses.[5] Scholars disagree, for example, about whether Cyrus worshiped the god Mithra or the Zoroastrian god Ahuramazda. It is difficult to know anything with certainty about ancient Persian religion.[6]

All we can say for certain is that Deutero-Isaiah admired Cyrus for political reasons: Cyrus freed the exiles from the yoke of Babylon. Consequently, YHWH could "anoint" Cyrus as someone who carried out his wishes, much as he had anointed the Aramean king Hazael (1 Kings 19:15;[7] see 2 Kings 8:13) and had regarded Nebuchadnezzar as his "servant" (Jeremiah 25:9, 43:10), though in none of these cases is there any reference to a religious influence.

The Judahites now faced the more favorable circumstances of the Persian empire, the largest empire the ancient Near East had ever known, extending from the Aegean Sea to the Indus River. Persian authorities seem to have shown respect for the many diverse local cultures and religions, at least as far as these peoples recognized the authority of the Great King. These conditions offered fertile soil for the development of a universal God.

CHAPTER 14

Israelite Religion in the Persian Empire: YHWH as "God of Heaven"

Biblical monotheism goes back to the mid-sixth century B.C.E., to the reign of the Babylonian king Nabonidus and to the prophet Deutero-Isaiah.[1] But such monotheism was not immediately and everywhere accepted, not in the increasingly diverse Jewish world of Judea, Samaria or the Diaspora.

In Babylonia, not all exiles took up Deutero-Isaiah's polemic, in which the Babylonian gods were reduced to nothing. Many exiles had adopted Babylonian customs, which involved tolerance for the local gods. A number of Israelites had names containing the theophoric elements of Mesopotamian gods, for example, Marduk or Nebo. It is difficult to make precise inferences about the beliefs of people with theophoric names, but it seems surprising, given the fierceness of Deutero-Isaiah's rhetoric, that the heroes of the Book of Esther—Esther herself and her cousin Mordecai—bear names derived from the Babylonian deities Ishtar and Marduk. It is thus likely that the nascent monotheism, for the most part, was not aggressive toward "idols" but rather tolerant of them, including the idols of the Babylonians as well as the idols of other peoples.

This attitude of accommodation also seems to characterize the Jewish community of Elephantine, an island in the Nile River in Upper Egypt (that is, southern Egypt). Aramaic papyri and ostraca[2] from Elephantine reveal that this community remained Yahwistic (they called YHWH "Yahô/YHW") while accepting a certain syncretism, generally related to intermarriage with Aramean or Egyptian spouses. It is in this context that we should understand blessing formulas by Yahô and an Egyptian divinity—"I blessed you by Yahô and [the Egyptian god of good fortune] Khn(um)" (ostracon Clermont-Ganneau 70.3)[3]—as well as an exculpatory oath sworn to an Aramean deity and Yahô: "Oath that Menahem son of Shallum son of Hôshaʻyah swore to Meshullam son of Natan ... by ʻAnat-Yaho."[4] The same applies to an oath uttered by a man named Malkiyah, who has a Yahwist name but is presented as an "Aramean," which explains the oath he delivered before a court: "I, Malkiyah, I witness against you to *Herem*/temenos[5] of Bethel, the god, among the four avengers."[6]

It is difficult to know how much these formulas, which were official utterances required for participation in various social activities (such as a law court), reflect the beliefs of those who used them. But cultural coexistence and mixed marriages probably reflect at least a measure of pragmatic tolerance.[7]

The need for accommodation with one's neighbors was certainly not limited to the Jewish colony on the island of Elephantine in the fifth century B.C.E. During the Roman period, the rabbis of the pharisaic tradition tried to specify what behaviors, in relationships with pagans, would be allowed or occasionally tolerated without becoming idolatry. Throughout the Jewish world, and especially in the Diaspora, Jews often had relationships with non-Jews simply in carrying on with daily life, and the famous Mishnah treatise *ʻAbodah Zarah* devotes five chapters to the risks of idolatry posed by such interactions.

For about two centuries after the Exile, from the mid-sixth century through the mid-fourth century B.C.E., the Near East was ruled by the Persian Achaemenid empire. This meant that Jewish priests and other leaders needed to communicate with their Persian overlords, which in turn meant being able to discuss their religious beliefs and practices with a people who followed Mazdaism. The Jewish leaders thus emphasized the transcendent and universal character of YHWH, which brought him closer to the great god Ahuramazda and made him understandable to the Persians. During the Persian period, YHWH is more and more frequently called by the general name "God," which could be understood in any culture, rather than by the specific name "YHWH," the name of the particular god of the Jews.

The use of such expressions is particularly clear in the Aramaic documents preserved in the Book of Ezra. (The Book of Ezra contains material from several sources, some dating earlier than Ezra himself, who was contemporaneous with the Persian king Artaxerxes II [c. 404-359 B.C.E.].)[8] In a letter to the Persian king Darius (c. 522-486 B.C.E.), Tattenai, governor of the province "Beyond the River" ("Tattenai" is also referred to in cuneiform inscriptions as governor of the province "Beyond the River"), describes the Temple of Jerusalem as "the house of the great God [bêit elâhâ' rabbâ']" (Ezra 5:8); and the Judeans helping to rebuild the temple are called "servants of the God of heaven and earth ['abdôhî dî-elâh shemayyâ' we'ar'â']" (Ezra 5:11). The decree of King Cyrus II (c. 559-530 B.C.E.) concerning the rebuilding of the Temple also employs the expression bêit elâhâ', "the house of God" (Ezra 6:3-5), which he specifies several times is "the God of heaven" (Ezra 6:9-10).

The Aramaic expression elâh shemayyâ' (the God of Heaven) is also attested in Jewish Aramaic texts from Elephantine (fifth century B.C.E.). These texts also frequently employ the proper name "Yahô/YHW"[9] (especially in letters exchanged between Jews), but elâh shemayyâ'[10] can easily be substituted for "Yahô/YHW." For example, a petition to the governor of Judea, a man named Bagohi, uses elâh shemayyâ' as well as "Yahô the God" and "Yahô the God of Heaven" to refer to YHWH;[11] the memorandum of the answer sent by the governor in response to the petition, however, uses only elâh shemayyâ'.[12]

YHWH is also referred to as elâh shemayyâ' in the firman (an official letter granting the bearer special privileges) issued to Ezra by the Persian king Artaxerxes II. This firman describes the so-called Ezra mission, which took place in the seventh year of Artaxerxes' reign, in 398

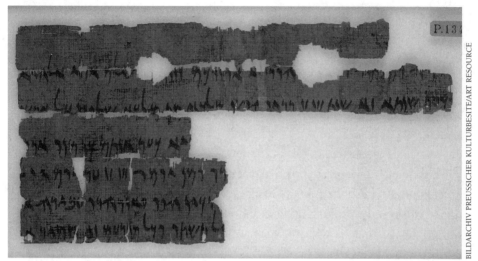

P.13

BILDARCHIV PREUSSICHER KULTURBESITE/ART RESOURCE

ELEPHANTINE PAPYRI. A Jewish community thrived on the island of Elephantine, on the Nile River, in the fifth century B.C.E. A trove of papyrus documents illuminates the life of the community; the document shown here is addressed to a Yedaniah from a certain Hananiah, who urges the Elephantine Jews to observe the Passover.

B.C.E.; it states that Ezra is to lead Jewish peoples scattered throughout Persian territories back to Jerusalem, taking with him the text of the Torah and vast resources dedicated to the Jerusalem Temple. In the firman, Ezra is officially called "the scribe of the law of the God of Heaven [*elâh shemayyâ'*]." In other words, the Torah brought from Babylonia by Ezra to codify the traditions and rites suitable for official Judaism is under the protection of the great universal God. Nevertheless, the Book of Ezra does reveal some tension between the old provincial Yahwism and the new universal Yahwism; sometimes the God of Israel is called "YHWH" and sometimes he is called "the God of Heaven."

In the firman, however, only the Aramaic expression *elâh shemayyâ'* (God of Heaven) is found (see Ezra 7:12,21-23) along with the expressions "God of Israel" (Ezra 7:15) and "God of Jerusalem" (Ezra 7:19). The tetragrammaton YHWH is completely lacking in this official letter. Henceforth "the God of Heaven" appears more and more frequently—initially in relations between non-Jews and Jews,[13] and then among Jews themselves—during the Persian period and the early Hellenistic period.

It also appears in the Book of Daniel (2:18-19,37,44; see also 2:28), while a Hebrew version (*elohey shamayim*) of the Aramaic *elâh shemayyâ'* appears in the books of Ezra (1:2) and Nehemiah (1:4-5, 2:4,20).[14]

A similar phenomenon was also taking place in contemporaneous Aramean civilization. The Canaanite storm god Baal was increasingly called Baal Shamayin/Baal Shamên[15] (Master of Heaven), as attested in Syria and Cilicia. In the Hellenistic period, Baal Shamayin was often considered another name for Zeus. On a fourth-century B.C.E. coin found at Samaria, for example, the Aramaic legend "Baal of Tarsus" (an avatar of Baal Shamayin[16]), used on Cilician coins, was replaced by the Greek legend "Zeus."[17] It may seem surprising that coins minted in Samaria would contain the name Zeus.

Such a "dialogue of the religions," or reciprocal influence among religions, seems to have developed during the Persian Achaemenid period. Recognition of the great gods of the various cultures did not prevent peoples from remaining attached to their own traditions and particular forms of worship, all with the blessing of Persian authorities. An example of this atmosphere of tolerance is the rebuilding of the Jerusalem Temple, concluded in 515 B.C.E. ("in the month of Adar the sixth year of the reign of King Darius" [Ezra 6:15]), and the restoration of certain types of sacrifices practiced in the first Temple.

In many ways, the inhabitants of the Persian province of Judea (called Judah in the First Temple period), who returned some 70 years after the 587 B.C.E. destruction of the Temple, retained a monolatrous faith with particularistic accents. Many of them wanted to restore an ideal Jewish nation in all its purity, and they often insisted on the importance of rites distinguishing Jews from other peoples—even from Jews who remained in Judah. This became a source of tension, not only between Jews who returned from Exile and Jews who did not, but also between the Jews of Judea and the Jews of neighboring provinces, such as Samaria.

Such tensions could be focused on places of worship. The destruction of the Jerusalem Temple, for example, probably involved the suspension of official sacrifices of animals. According to the Book of Jeremiah, however, "On the day after the murder of [the Babylonian-appointed governor] Gedaliah ... eighty men arrived from Shechem and Shiloh and Samaria, with their beards shaved and their clothes torn, and their bodies gashed, bringing grain offerings and incense to present at the temple of YHWH" (Jeremiah 41:4-5). As we have no evidence of a temple at Gedaliah's capital of Mizpah,[18] the temple here is probably the temple of Jerusalem, which now lay in ruins. Apparently rituals involving vegetable offerings, rather than animal sacrifices, continued to be performed at the site of the Temple. Animal offerings were not restored until the return of the first exiles, probably around 538/537 B.C.E. (see Ezra 3). The rebuilding of the temple in 515 B.C.E. allowed for a complete resumption of the rites and sacrifices performed before the fall of Jerusalem (Ezra 6:15).

Unfortunately, we have no certain information about any temple of YHWH built in Babylonia, or about any rites and sacrifices that may have been performed in Exile. The prophet Ezekiel, however, may refer to the existence of a small temple: "Though I removed them far away among the nations, and though I scattered them among the countries, yet I have been a sanctuary to them for a little while in the countries where they have gone" (Ezekiel 11:16).[19] Indeed, one of the purposes of Ezekiel's preaching was to convince the Israelites that the divine presence remained with them in Exile, despite the destruction of the Jerusalem Temple.[20]

We know more about cult practices outside of Babylonia. Not only did the Judeans have a Yahwist temple in Jerusalem (after 515 B.C.E.), but so did the Samaritans, on Mount Gerizim,[21] and the Idumeans, probably at Khirbet el-Qom/Makkedah.[22] We have also seen that the Jews of Elephantine, in Upper Egypt, had a temple of Yahô.

From the correspondence of the Jews of Elephantine with the high priest of Jerusalem and the governors of Judea and Samaria, it appears that the high priest in Jerusalem did not answer and that the governors gave only reluctant authorization—with great initial misgiving[23] and a number of reservations—for the rebuilding of the temple of Yahô at Elephantine. According to a memorandum written around 407 B.C.E., the governors of Judea and Samaria gave the community permission to make vegetable offerings and to use incense, but not to sacrifice animals:

Regarding the house of the altar (*byt mdbḥ*) of the God of heaven
in Elephantine-the-fortress, built before the reign of Cambyses

and destroyed in the year 14 of King Darius by the criminal Vidranga: Build it in its place as it was before, and plant offerings and incense are to be presented on this altar (*wmnht' wlbwnt' yqrbwn 'l mdbh zk*) in accordance with what was before.[24]

By the end of the fifth century B.C.E., then, official doctrine appears to have limited the sacrifice of animals to the Jerusalem Temple but allowed for plant and incense offerings elsewhere.

The biblical scholar Alfred Marx has suggested that the influence of Persian religion accounts for the vegetable offerings in the Bible, especially in the P (Priestly) strand of the Pentateuch. According to Marx, "It is not thus excessive to think that through this official sacrifice P met the Zoroastrian ideal of non-violence and respect of life, the echoes of which had already reached him by the preaching of Deutero-Isaiah [see Isaiah 11:6-9, 65:25]."[25]

Perhaps not surprisingly, the evolution of vegetable and incense offerings, especially in the Diaspora, probably made Yahwism more acceptable to foreign populations, as the Book of Malachi implies: "For from the rising of the sun to its setting my name is great among the nations, and in every place incense is offered to my name, and a pure offering" (Malachi 1:11).

During the Exile, then, a movement developed that strictly regulated sacrificial worship, especially the sacrifice of animals. Thus the prophet Hosea quotes YHWH, "I desire steadfast love (*hesed*) and not sacrifice (*zabah*), the knowledge of God rather than burnt offerings" (Hosea 6:6). Such thinking could well have led to the notion that the Temple itself, while a good and holy place, was not necessary:

Thus says YHWH:
Heaven is my throne
and the earth is my footstool;
what is the house that you would build for me,
and what is my resting place?
(Isaiah 66:1).[26]

It is probably in the context of this relativization of sacrifice (see also

1 Samuel 15:22-23; Amos 5:22,25; Hosea 8:13; Isaiah 1:11; and Jeremiah 6:20, 7:1-8:3)[27] and the emphasis on the "knowledge of God" that we should understand the birth of the synagogue.

CHAPTER 15

The Temple, the Synagogue and Absolute Aniconism

Despite much research, the origins of the synagogue remain obscure.[1] Some scholars propose that synagogues first sprung up during the Babylonian Exile, as part of a tradition of prayer and study that developed around exiled priests, prophets and scribes.[2] To date, however, we have no literary, epigraphical or archaeological evidence for synagogues in Babylonia during the Exilic period.

The oldest Jewish synagogues, or gathering houses, are called *proseuchè* (Greek for "place of prayer") or *proseuchè Ioudaiōn* ("place of prayer of the Jews"). The term *proseuchè* was never applied to a non-Jewish building,[3] and sometimes the *proseuchè* was dedicated to *hypsistō theō* (God Most High).[4] These "places of prayer" are attested in third-century B.C.E. Greek inscriptions from the Egyptian Fayum, about 40 miles southwest of Cairo. The term "synagogue" (from the Greek *synagōgè*, meaning "assembly" or "place of assembly") appears in the Fayum later, replacing the term *proseuchè* by the second century C.E.

Significantly, the earliest epigraphical evidence of synagogues comes from the Diaspora: an inscription from the reign of Ptolemy III Euergetes (246-221 B.C.E.) from Arsinoe (Crocodilopolis) in the Fayum;[5] another inscription dated to the reign of Ptolemy III from Schedia in Lower Egypt (Northern Egypt);[6] a papyrus dated 218 B.C.E. from Alexandrou-Nesos in Middle Egypt;[7] and inscriptions from the second and first centuries B.C.E. from several sites in the Nile Delta, including Xenephyris,[8] Athribis,[9] Nitriai[10] and Alexandria.[11] A first-century B.C.E synagogue on the Aegean island of Delos reveals that the phenomenon extended to the eastern Mediterranean,[12] and some first-century B.C.E. inscriptions indicate that synagogues even existed in Rome.[13]

This epigraphical evidence confirms what we know from the literary tradition. Around the turn of the era, according to Philo, Josephus and the New Testament, there were synagogues throughout the eastern Mediterranean. Moreover, an inscription on a recently published ossuary (a bone-box used for secondary burials) indicates that synagogues also existed in the Syrian interior, in Apamea and Palmyra.[14]

The earliest synagogues in Palestine itself come somewhat later, and for years scholars debated whether any existed before the year 70 C.E., when the Romans destroyed the Herodian Temple. The absence of archaeological and epigraphical evidence was surprising, given references in the Gospels to synagogues in the Galilee; and according to later rabbinical tradition, numerous synagogues also existed in Jerusalem. Since the 1960s, however, several pre-70 C.E. synagogues have been found, for example at Masada and Herodion. But the only inscription from a pre-70 C.E. Palestinian synagogue was found during excavations in the area of Jerusalem known as the City of David in 1913-1914. This first-century C.E. inscription,[15] incised in Greek on a limestone slab 25 inches wide and 17 inches high, specifies the functions of a synagogue at that time:[16]

Theodotus son of Vettenus, priest and synagogue leader, son of a synagogue leader, grandson of a synagogue leader, rebuilt this synagogue for the reading of the Law and the teaching of the commandments, and the hostelry, rooms and baths, for the lodging of those who have need from abroad. It was established by his forefathers, the elders and Simonides.

"THEODOTUS ... priest and synagogue leader ... rebuilt this synagogue for the reading of the Law and the teaching of the commandments," reads a first-century C.E. Greek inscription found in Jerusalem. The fact that the text is in Greek, not Hebrew, and its reference to "those who have need from abroad," suggests that the synagogue was used by Jews from the Diaspora and that it housed large numbers of visiting pilgrims. Some scholars have identified it with the Synagogue of the Freedmen (former slaves in the Roman Empire), mentioned in Acts 6:9.

Even if Theodotus's synagogue served as a hostelry and ritual bath (*miqveh*) for pilgrims, its primary function was as a venue for the reading and teaching of the Law. Thus it resembled the *beit midrash* ("house of instruction") referred to in the Book of Ecclesiasticus 51:23. The *beit midrash*, however, was apparently a place of study for younger students, whereas the purpose of the synagogue was to have the Law read for all. In the synagogue, the scriptures were studied by everyone, as a kind of continuing weekly education. The first-century C.E. historian Josephus—a Jew from a priestly Jerusalem family who wrote histories in Aramaic and Greek while living in Rome—describes this kind of study:

[Moses] appointed the Law to be the most excellent and necessary form of instruction, ordaining, not that it should be heard

once or twice or on several occasions, but that every week men should desert their other occupations and assemble to listen to the Law and to obtain a thorough and accurate knowledge of it (*Against Apion* 2.175).

From excavations at Masada, Herodion, Magdala, Gamla, Kiriat-Sefer[17] and, perhaps, Capernaum[18] and Jericho,[19] we know a good deal about the architecture of Palestinian synagogues. They were clearly built as gathering places, consisting of a large hall where members could sit on benches. There was no altar and no cella (holy niche).

Did the institution of the synagogue change between the third century B.C.E. and 70 C.E.? The evidence strongly indicates that these "places of prayer" had their origins in the Diaspora and later spread to Palestine and to Jerusalem itself. It seems likely, then, that their impetus in Palestine came from the Diaspora; that is, Jewish pilgrims would have spread the word that synagogues could be built to teach the Law. Perhaps the first synagogues in Palestine were even built by Jews returning to Israel from the Diaspora—which would explain why the Theodotus Inscription was written in Greek. (Some scholars have identified the synagogue of the Theodotus Inscription with the "synagogue of the Freedmen" mentioned in the Book of Acts 6:9).[20] The Jews of Jerusalem were late to adopt the institution of the synagogue probably because the Temple precinct itself served as a place to read and teach the Law.

The fact that synagogues took root in Judea somewhat slowly reflects the history of the region. Until the beginning of the Hasmonean period (141-37 B.C.E.), Judea was a relatively small territory, extending no more than 20 miles from Jerusalem, so that Judeans could easily travel to Jerusalem to worship at the Temple. Not until 112/111 B.C.E. were Idumea, in the south, and Samaria, in the north,[21] annexed to the Hasmonean kingdom by John Hyrcanus; and only in 104/103 B.C.E. did central Galilee become part of the Jewish kingdom, with its capital in Jerusalem. The problem of Jews living at a distance from Jerusalem, therefore, only arose around 100 B.C.E. for the "new" Jews of southern and northern Palestine, who might then have needed local community centers. This scenario regarding the evolution of the synagogue remains only a hypothesis, however, and more evidence is needed to confirm or refute it.

What is clear is that the synagogue, depending on where it was, could appear first as a house of prayer (Egypt) or as a house of study (Israel). In fact, it seems likely that these two functions of the synagogue were combined in synagogues before 70 C.E., and that both were part of the weekly synagogue liturgy as described by Josephus. In this liturgy, the writings of the Torah and the Prophets played a paramount role.

The institution of the synagogue is characteristic of a "religion of the book," not a religion of sacrifices. With the development of synagogues, sacrifices continued to be performed, but only within the framework of the Jerusalem Temple. The Temple continued to be an important pilgrimage center, attracting visitors from Israel and the Diaspora. It was an awesome and imposing institution with its complicated ritual ceremonies, its priestly hierarchies, its sacrifices of animals and grain. This Temple was entirely rebuilt—and on what a scale, with its earthen platform forming a rough rectangle of some 1,600 feet by 900 feet—by Herod the Great, who made it one of the most spectacular monuments of the eastern Roman Empire.[22] Through its architecture and its sacrifices, the Herodian Temple could compete with the most elaborate pagan temples of the day. It was the religious and national reference point of Judaism at the turn of the era, and it prolonged the ancestral Yahwist tradition by maintaining the priesthood and sacrifices. The Temple had so high a reputation in the Roman Empire that, as the Alexandrian Jewish scholar Philo recalled, Augustus himself "ordered that burnt sacrifices be offered at his expense everyday to the God Most High (hypsistô theô), and this institution has remained in force so far."[23]

Even if the Herodian Temple was partly inspired by the architecture of pagan temples, and even if the Temple's priests regularly performed sacrifices to YHWH in honor of the Roman emperor, it remained strictly a part of the national cult. Non-Jews were prohibited from entering the holy precinct of the Temple, under penalty of death—as we know from two Greek Herodian inscriptions, which describe the parapet separating the pagan court from the sacred enclosure.[24] The exclusion of pagans from the holy part of the Jerusalem Temple goes back at least to the time

THE PROPHET SAMUEL (left) anoints David (center) king of Israel, as painted on the wall of a third-century C.E. synagogue at Dura-Europos, in modern Syria. In the mid-third century, Dura, a fortress on the eastern edge of the Roman Empire, supported a multi-ethnic community that practiced a variety of religions. At the beginning of the Christian era, author Lemaire notes, synagogues welcomed not only jews but also non-jews who "feared God."

ART RESOURCE, NY

of Antiochus III (223-187 B.C.E.), who, according to Josephus, recognized that it was "forbidden for any foreigner to enter the enclosure of the Temple."[25]

According to one of the Dead Sea Scrolls (4QFlorilegium), those excluded from the holy precinct of the Temple included not only Ammonites and Moabites but also children of illegitimate marriages (*mamzerim*), foreigners and proselytes (*gerim*).[26] Around 58 C.E. the Apostle Paul was seized by an angry mob for having "brought Greeks into the temple ... and defiled this holy place" (Acts 21:28). Moreover, the First Jewish Revolt of 66-70 B.C.E. (with Masada holding out for a few years afterward) was precipitated by the strict enforcement of this exclusion and the cessation of sacrifices offered for the emperor. According to Josephus, "Eleazar, son of Ananias the high priest, a very daring youth, then holding the position of captain, persuaded those who officiated in the Temple services to accept no gift or sacrifice from a foreigner. This action laid the foundation of the war with the Romans."[27] Paradoxically, then, it was the strict exclusion of foreigners from the Temple that led to the destruction of the Temple itself.

Synagogues, on the other hand, at least in the Diaspora, appear to have been more open and inviting. Synagogues seem to have been accessible to anyone who "feared god," whether Jew or non-Jew (see the Acts of the Apostles 10:1-22, 13:16-26, 16:14, 18:7).[28]

One practice in synagogues that made them more open to non-Jews was the tendency to refer to the God of Israel not as "YHWH" but as the "Most High" (hypsistos),[29] which could also refer to Zeus,[30] to a great Phoenician deity[31] or to other gods worshiped by non-Jews. This is a reversal of the development that occurred toward the beginning of the first millennium B.C.E., when the divine name 'Elyon (Most High) became replaced by "YHWH"; now, beginning around 200 B.C.E. and continuing through the Hellenistic and Roman periods, "YHWH" tends to be replaced by the appellative "Most High." A Greek translation of the Book of Ecclesiasticus from the second half of the second century B.C.E., for example, uses the word hypsistos about 50 times to refer to God and the tetragrammaton does not appear at all in the Masada fragments.[32] The Aramaic 'Ilayâ' (Most High) appears frequently in the Book of Daniel (3:26, 4:2,24,25,32,34, 5:18,21, 7:25; see also 7:18,22,25,27), and the Greek hypsistos often appears in the works of Luke (Luke 1:32,35,76, 6:35, 8:28; Acts 7:48, 16:17).

Although the synagogue was a more accessible and fluid institution than the Jerusalem Temple, the Temple too could mean different things to different groups.[33] We have already seen that during and after the Exile, rituals once reserved for the Temple (especially after the reforms of Hezekiah and Josiah), such as offerings of grain or incense, could now be performed in such places as Babylon or Elephantine. Or sacrificial rituals could be dropped entirely, with Yahwists urged to know and love and fear God rather than to make offerings to him.

According to Josephus, the Essenes send "votive offerings to the temple but [do not?][34] perform sacrifices,[35] employing a different ritual of purification. This is why they are barred from those precincts of the Temple that are frequented by all the people and perform their rites by themselves"[36] (the authenticity of this passage is disputed by some scholars). Although the attitude of the Essenes toward the Jerusalem Temple remains somewhat ambiguous,[37] it is clear that they did not take part in the cult as practiced by the high priests of Jerusalem.

Furthermore, the site of Qumran on the northwest coast of the Dead Sea, with its buildings and library, was probably a kind of Essene *beit midrash* (house of study) deliberately located at a distance from Jerusalem and its Temple.[38] Under these circumstances, the Essenes "spiritualized" sacrificial worship; the "offering of lips," or praise of God, replaced the offering of sacrifices. This is confirmed by Philo, who recounts that the Essenes were "devoted to the service of God not by offering sacrifices of animals but by resolving to sanctify their minds."[39]

In the first half of the first century C.E., another group adopted a somewhat ambivalent attitude toward the Temple: the "sect of the Nazarenes," as Jesus and his early followers are called in the Acts 24:5. Some texts, particularly the work of Luke, show Jesus and his disciples attending the Jerusalem Temple like anyone else. Other texts, however, express skepticism and even hostility toward the Temple, its rituals and its priests, such as the account of Jesus' driving the money-changers from the Temple (Matthew 21:12-13; Mark 11:15-17; Luke 19:45-46; John 2:13-17),[40] Jesus' prophecies regarding the destruction of the Temple (Matthew 24,2-3,26,61 and parallels), and the speech by Stephen (one of the leaders of the Jerusalem church) stating that "the Most High does not live in houses made with human hands" (Acts 7:48; see also 6:13-14).[41]

Nonetheless, one important feature of the Jerusalem Temple remained in place until its final destruction in 70 C.E., a feature that distinguished the Jerusalem temple from all contemporaneous pagan temples: the emptiness of the cella, or Holy of Holies.[42] In describing the Romans' entry into Jerusalem in 63 B.C.E., the Roman historian Tacitus makes note of this odd fact:

Pompey was the first Roman who overcame the Jews and who, by right of conquest, penetrated into the temple. At this point in time the rumor spread that the temple contained no figure of gods, that the sanctuary was empty and did not hide any mystery.[43]

The utter emptiness of the Temple's sanctum sanctorum is confirmed by Josephus: "The innermost recess measured twenty cubits, and was separated off by a screen. Inside stood nothing whatever: Unapproachable, inviolable, invisible to all, it was called the Holy of Holies."[44]

This absolute aniconism of the Jews and their Temple is mentioned relatively frequently in classical sources. The late-fourth-century B.C.E. Greek ethnographer Hecataeus of Abdera attributed Jewish aniconism to Moses, who allowed "no images whatsoever of the gods ... being of the opinion that God is not in human form.[45] The late-first-century B.C.E. Roman historian Strabo, probably relying on the work of Posidonius of Apamea (c. 145-85 B.C.E.),[46]also discussed the Mosaic concept of divinity and worship:

Which judicious man would dare to represent this divinity by an image made on the model of one of us? It is thus necessary to give up any manufacture of statues and to be limited, to honor the divinity, to dedicate a sacred enclosure and a sanctuary to him worthy of him, without any effigy.[47]

Another Roman historian, Tacitus, who lived in the second half of the first century C.E., also commented on this unusual aspect of the religion of the Jews:

The Jews conceive the divinity only in thought and admit only one [God]. For them it is a profanation to make images of the gods with perishable materials and to the resemblance of man. To their eyes, the supreme being is eternal, inimitable, impossible to destroy. Thus they do not have any representation of him in their cities or in their temples.[48]

Much more familiar to ancient visitors were the traditional Temple sacrifices. Even if these sacrifices, offered by priests, constituted the principal ritual activity of the Temple, the precinct also served both as a "house of prayer"[49] and as a place for teaching the Law. Masters and disciples could gather there in the shade of the porticoes surrounding its esplanade (see Luke 2:46, 21:37; Acts 2:46, 5:12,20,21,42). In other words, the kinds of activities associated with synagogues—especially the effort to learn the divine Law and to know God—had spread even to the High Place of the thousand-year-old Yahwist sacrificial cult: the Temple of Jerusalem.

CHAPTER 16
The Disappearance of YHWH

B y the first century B.C.E. Yahwism had become completely aniconic. It had also, in a sense, ceased to be Yahwism, for the name
YHWH had virtually disappeared as a proper name of the divinity.

When the Israelites returned from Exile, they needed to be able to
communicate with the various representatives of the immense Persian
empire, including the Persian overlords themselves. This led to a dimin-
ishment of the particularity of the God of Israel and to a less frequent
use of the name "YHWH/YHW," which often came to be replaced, especially in Aramaic, by *elâh shemayyâ'* (the God of Heaven). This practice
of substituting "the God of Heaven" for "YHWH" quickly became widespread in Hebrew writings as well.

The name "YHWH" does not appear in the late biblical literature. It
is conspicuously absent from the Book of Job, the Song of Songs, Eccle-
siastes and Esther.[1] Even though the reason for YHWH's absence may
differ from book to book, it is striking to note that they are generally late
books, from the Persian or even Hellenistic period.

In substituting other theonyms for YHWH, Jews were probably also
seeking to obey biblical law in the strictest possible manner.

One of the commands of the Decalogue involves the use of the divine name: "You shall not make wrongful use of the name of YHWH your God, for YHWH will not acquit anyone who misuses his name" (Exodus 20:7). Originally, this commandment was likely intended to prohibit false oaths (see Leviticus 19:12), especially in the context of a treaty or a lawsuit. Pre-Exilic literature and Hebrew inscriptions often tend to invoke YHWH by pronouncing his name, a phenomenon also attested in the fifth-century B.C.E.[2] But the commandment was later interpreted as prohibiting utterance of the name "YHWH" in everyday life. It is possible that one reason for this prohibition was to prevent the divine Name from being used in divination or magic,[3] as seen in some ancient magic intaglios[4] and several psalms of exorcism found among the Dead Sea Scrolls at Qumran (such as 11Q11).[5]

Whatever the reasons, toward the end of the Hellenistic period[6] and during the Roman period, Jews, especially Jews of the Diaspora[7] but probably also Jews living in Judea, avoided pronouncing the name "YHWH." In reading the old religious texts that came to form the Bible, they replaced "YHWH" with the reverential Hebrew title "Adonai," which the Greeks translated as *kyrios* (Master/Lord).

The course of this evolution is difficult to trace precisely. In the oldest manuscripts of the Septuagint (for example, in papyrus 4QLXXLev B),[8] the Greek transcription "IAÔ" is used, while in other manuscripts (for example, papyrus Fouad 266),[9] the tetragrammaton is neither translated nor transcribed in Greek but retained in Judean Aramaic script. This preservation of the Judean Aramaic tetragrammaton is then adapted into Greek as "PIPI."[10] Other Judean Greek manuscripts present the tetragrammaton in paleo-Hebrew script.[11] Finally, especially in manuscripts transmitted by the Christian tradition,[12] YHWH is written as *kyrios,* which implies that these texts were based on original Hebrew manuscripts in which the tetragrammaton was rendered as "Adonai."

The discovery of the Qumran manuscripts—or Dead Sea Scrolls—a little more than half a century ago shed new light on ancient usage of the tetragrammaton. These manuscripts are mainly Hebrew or Aramaic texts copied between the end of the third century B.C.E. and 68 C.E. The appearance of the tetragrammaton in these texts is dependent on chronology (it becomes more rare the later the text) and, possibly, on

differences among scribal schools (the most significant school represented
was the Qumran school, which many scholars believe was Essene) or even
among individual scribes.[13] The Dead Sea Scrolls show at least a dozen ways
of transcribing the tetragrammaton:[14]

1. It can be transcribed with the same characters (in paleo-
Hebrew or in square Judean Aramaic/Hebrew) as the remainder
of the manuscript.[15]

2. The tetragrammaton is not written at all on the line but five
supralinear dots above the following word presumably indicate
the reading "Adonai/Lord": 1QIsa[a] XXXV,15 (= 42, 6).

3. In a significant number of square Hebrew texts, the tetragrammaton is written in paleo-Hebrew, probably to indicate that it was
not to be pronounced, unlike the remainder of the text. This practice seems to be widely used in the scribal school of Qumran.[16]

4. In ten manuscripts,[17] particularly texts devoted to the rules of
the Qumran sect,[18] the tetragrammaton is replaced by four points
suspended from the line of writing of the other letters.[19] These
manuscripts were apparently copied between the second half of
the second century B.C.E. and about the middle of the first century B.C.E. They are characteristic of the scribal school of Qumran, and four of them were likely copied by the same scribe.[20]

5. Some texts replace the tetragrammaton, especially in biblical
quotations, with 'DNY (Adonai).[21]

6. In a few texts, the tetragrammaton is replaced by 'L (God).[22]
This is the reverse of the early first-millennium B.C.E. practice of
replacing "El" with "YHWH."

7. In 4Q364 (Pentateuchal Paraphrase), the tetragrammaton is
written in square Hebrew characters but preceded by two vertical

points, perhaps to alert the reader to the special quality of this word.[23]

8. Many Qumran texts, in Hebrew and Aramaic, replace the tetragrammaton with 'LYWN (Elyon/Most High) or 'L 'LYWN (El Elyon/El, God Most High).[24]

9. In manuscript 4Q248 (4QHistorical Text A),[25] the tetragrammaton is replaced by five strokes.

10. In 11Q22 (11QpaleoUnidentified Text),[26] L'LHYK ("to your God") is written with an ink of a different color than the remainder of the manuscript.[27]

11. In 4Q511 10:12, YWD seems to be substituted for YHWH (see Psalm 19:10).[28]

12: In 1QS 8:13, HW'H seems to be substituted for YHWH (see Isaiah 40:3).

Besides these various practices,[29] the rule of the Qumran community absolutely prohibited pronouncing the divine name. Transgressing this rule meant expulsion from the community:

> Whoever pronounces the name honored (YZKR DBR BŠM HNKBD) over all ... by surprise when confronted by misfortune ('M QLL 'W LHB'H MṢRH) or for any other reason ... or if he reads in a book or if he blesses, then he will be excluded and he will not return any more to the council of the community (1QS VI, 27-vii, 2).[30]

This severe prohibition against pronouncing the tetragrammaton was not confined to the Essene movement. From the acceptance of the Torah of Ezra, this prohibition was probably related to the solemn judgment against blasphemy, codified in Leviticus 24:10-26. In Leviticus 24:16 of the Septuagint (composed in Alexandria around the mid-third century B.C.E.), the prohibition against blasphemy is already generalized to forbid pronunciation of the divine Name (*en tô onomasai auton to onoma kyriou*).[31]

Before the destruction of the Temple by the Romans in 70 C.E., there was only a single exception to the prohibition against uttering the divine name: the high priest in the Temple.[32] In the Book of Ecclesiasticus, for example, the high priest Simon blesses Israelites gathered at the Temple:

> Then Simon came down and raised his hands
> over the whole congregation of Israelites,
> to pronounce the blessing of the Lord with his lips,
> and to glory in his name;
> and they bowed down in worship a second time
> to receive the blessing from the Most High.
> (Ecclesiasticus 50:20-21)[33]

According to the Mishnah, only the high priest could pronounce the tetragrammaton in its correct intonation, and even then only in the Temple on Yom Kippur (*Yoma* 3:8, 4:2, 6:2; see *Tamid* 3:8). The high priest was also the only one on that day who could enter the Temple's Holy of Holies, where he could recite the sacerdotal blessing and pronounce "the Name such as it is written" (*Sotah* 7:6; *Tamid* 7:2; see Jerusalem Talmud, *Yoma* 3:7). To some extent, then, the high priest was the last witness— around the turn of the era—of Israelite Yahwism, and the Temple was the last refuge of the worship of YHWH as a particular divinity.

When the Romans captured Jerusalem and destroyed the Temple, in 70 C.E., the animal sacrifices performed in the Temple became a thing of the past, as did the role of the high priests (and the influence of the Sadducee movement). This also marked the end of Israelite Yahwism, since the particular Name of the God of Israel could no longer be pronounced, not generally or in religious practice.[34] Josephus (who was from a priestly family)[35] recognized that he was forbidden from pronouncing the divine name[36] and used the Greek term *despotès* (Sovereign Lord) as an equivalent of the tetragrammaton.[37] In the Mishnah tractate *Sanhedrin,* among the lists of "those who will not have a share in the

THE DEAD SEA SCROLL known as the Habakkuk Commentary shows how some ancient Jewish scribes treated the divine name. When this scroll's scribe came to the name of the deity, he wrote out the tetragrammaton-the four-letter personal name of God—in archaic, slanted paleo-Hebrew script, rather than in the square script of the rest of the text. Two examples can be seen on this fragment. In line 7, the third word from the right, one can see the four letters of the tetragrammaton (*yod, heh, vav, heh*) in a quotation from Habakkuk 2:13. The letters appear again in the last complete line, the second word from the left, in a quotation from Habakkuk 2:14. The verse reads: "For the earth will be filled with the knowledge of the Lord, as the waters cover the sea."

world to come," Abba Saul includes "the one who pronounces the Name with its proper letters" (10:1). Abba Saul, who lived after the year 70, did not make any exceptions, not even for the high priest on Yom Kippur. In fact, the tetragrammaton does not appear in the Mishnah, except under the abbreviation YY,[38] and the Greek transcription IAÔ is absent from the New Testament.[39]

The disappearance of YHWH, especially in prayer and worship, gives emphasis to the transcendental character of the divinity. The transcendent oneness of God is indicated in the designations used to evoke Him: Lord/Master, Most High/Supreme. He is the God of Everywhere and All, not just of the Temple and the people of Israel. The destruction of the Herodian Temple meant the end of Yahwism as a particular religion related to YHWH.[40] Judaism was now a religion of universal monotheism.

This monotheism, as we have seen, was a complex phenomenon that evolved over some 1,400 years. Its evolution was especially characterized by two developments:

First, Yahwism, a local cult in the southern desert around the 13th century B.C.E., developed into an Israelite monolatry. Over time YHWH became the exclusive God of the Israelites, to the exclusion of all foreign gods. This movement reached its apogee with the reform of Josiah at the end of the seventh century B.C.E., when, according to the epigraphical record, there was a dramatic increase in the proportion of Yahwist names.

Second, the national religion of Yahwism was thrown into a crisis with the Babylonian Exile—that is, with the collapse of Judah and the resettlement of Judahites in Babylonia. This event could well have marked the end of Yahwism as a monolatry (with YHWH, the God of Israel, defeated by the gods of Babylonia). Thanks to the prophets, however, monolatrous Yahwism was transformed into a universal monotheism; this is attested in Deutero-Isaiah's prophecies from the mid-sixth century B.C.E.

The transformation from monolatry into monotheism was probably partly related to the new international context in which the Judahite exiles found themselves: They no longer lived in the place of Yahweh (Israel/Jerusalem), and they needed to show deference to the local divinities. Yahwism was kept alive—in a transcendental, monotheistic form—by the strong sense of religious feeling among the Israelites prior to and then during the Exile. Also, the fact that their worship was aniconic—meaning that YHWH was not localized by images of him placed in his temples—allowed Yahwism to be transportable. YHWH's presence, the presence of the God Most High, could even be felt by the waters of Babylon.

When Yahwism became the national religion of Israel, worship was centralized in the Jerusalem Temple, with its complex and strictly governed sacrificial ceremonies. Ultimately, this led to the multiplication of places of prayer—in synagogues, with non-sacrificial worship based on praise and study of Scripture.

As it was being transformed into a universal monotheism, Yahwism opened itself to other peoples, spread outside the old territories of Israel and Judah, and disappeared as a particular form of worship with the fall of the Temple in 70 C.E. Yahwism, that is to say, fulfilled its historical role by giving birth to universal monotheism.

The Pronunciation of the Tetragrammaton "YHWH"

The earliest evidence of the tetragrammaton, the four consonants representing the name YHWH, the God of Israel, is found on the Mesha Stela (Moabite Stone), which dates to the second half of ninth century B.C.E. On this stela, the Moabite king Mesha describes the longstanding confrontation between Moab (the land directly east of the Dead Sea) and Israel as a confrontation between their two national deities: Chemosh and YHWH. The tetragrammaton later appears in Hebrew inscriptions from Kuntillet ʿAjrud and Khirbet el-Qom, dating to the eighth century B.C.E., and on ostraca (inscribed potsherds) from Lachish and Arad, dating to the late seventh and early sixth centuries B.C.E.

At least twice in inscriptions from Kuntillet ʿAjrud, and frequently in Aramaic documents from Elephantine (fifth century B.C.E.), the tetragrammaton is shortened to only three letters, YHW. This reduction to three letters also appears as a theophoric element in names from the southern kingdom of Judah during the First Temple period. Inscriptions from the northern kingdom of Israel simplify the tetragrammaton to YW.

According to the Bible, the proper name of the God of Israel is revealed to Moses. God tells Moses: "Thus you shall say to the Israelites, 'YHWH ... has sent me to you': This is my name forever, and this my title for all generations" (Exodus 3:15).

Do we know with any certainty how to pronounce this theonym?

The exact pronunciation of the tetragrammaton is very difficult to specify because the Jews of the Hellenistic and Roman periods avoided pronouncing the tetragrammaton and replaced it with the reverential Hebrew title "Adonai" ("Master/Lord"). In the Septuagint, a Greek translation of the Hebrew Bible dating to the third and second century B.C.E., Adonai is for the most part translated as *kyrios;* and God is called *kyrios* in the New Testament Greek. Later, around sixth century C.E., the rabbis who produced the Masoretic vocalization of the Hebrew Bible gave the tetragrammaton the vowels of the word "Adonai." This has been interpreted as meaning that the divine name is pronounced YeHoWaH,[1] but it really means that one should not pronounce the tetragrammaton at all; instead, one should substitute the honorific "Adonai."

How did one pronounce the tetragrammaton before the fourth century B.C.E., before the Hellenistic period? It is impossible to say with certainty because, in the earlier period, only consonants were written. As a result there are three possibilities: "Yahwoh," "Yahweh" and "Yahwa."

The argument for "Yahwoh" is based on two characteristics of paleo-Hebrew orthography. First, during the period of the monarchy, the consonant "H" is often preceded by the vowel "O," particularly in marking the third person singular (*ahu>oh*), as in the name "Neboh" (in later Hebrew, the third person singular is denoted by a simple "W"). Second, in the proper names of this period, the divine name is generally shortened to YW (pronounced *yawo>yaw?*) in the northern kingdom or to YHW (pronounced *yahwo>yâhu?*) in the Judahite kingdom. Since the sound "O" is often associated with the semi-consonant "W," the tetragrammaton could well have been pronounced "Yahwoh."

"Yahwoh" evolved into YHW/yâhu as a theophoric element in Judahite proper names (with the loss of the final "H") and into YW

Yaw/Yau in the kingdom of Israel (with the loss of both "H"s). This vocalization may be based on the Egyptian word *Y-H-W3-W,* found in an inscription on the wall of a temple built by Amenhotep III (c. 1390-1353) at Soleb in Nubia; the final "W" can indicate that the preceding group be pronounced *wo.*[2] Moreover, "Yahwoh" is in harmony with the vocalization of the Greek transcription *IAÔ,*[3] as well as with the later Latin form, *IAHO,* used by the church father Jerome.[4]

The argument for the pronunciation "Yahweh" rests on an interpretation of the meaning of the name. In the biblical account, the revelation of the tetragrammaton is associated with the Hebrew verb "to be" (*hāwāh/hāyāh*):

Moses said to God: "If I come to the Israelites and say to them, 'The God of your ancestors has sent me to you,' and they ask me, 'What is his name?' what shall I say to them?" God said to Moses, "I am who I am [*'èheyèh 'ashèr 'èheyèh*]." He said further, "Thus you shall say to the Israelites, 'I am has sent me to you'" (Exodus 3:13-14).

This answer is sometimes interpreted as God's refusing to reveal his name, sometimes as God's stating that the God of Israel is the only god who "is" (that is, the other gods do not exist), and sometimes as God's making clear his intention to serve as the God of his people: "I am who I will be," or "I will reveal myself in action, in being at your side." Such a threefold interpretation could explain the vocalization of the tetragrammaton as "Yahweh,"[5] which could mean "he causes to be." As such, God does not provide his name but his attributes. "Yahweh" is also consistent with such Greek transcriptions of the tetragrammaton as *Iaoue/ai* in Clement of Alexandria (late second century C.E.),[6] *Iabe* in Epiphanius (fourth century C.E.)[7] and *Iabe/Iabai* among the Samaritans (fifth century C.E.).[8]

The argument for "Yahwa" is based on the transcription of theophoric Yahwist names into Babylonian Akkadian around 500 B.C.E. (*yâhû* or *yâma,* probably pronounced *yâwa*)[9] The theophoric element *yâhû,* however, could also come from the nominative form *yâhwû/yâhwoh.*[10] Moreover, around 500 B.C.E., under the probable influence of Aramaic, one could expect a change of a final "o" into "a."

In all probability, the theonym YHWH was originally pronounced "Yahwoh."[11] The "Yahweh" pronunciation later became widespread, to give a theological interpretation to the mysterious, ancient name "YHWH," which may have initially been a place-name.

Endnotes

NOTES TO CHAPTER 1

[1] See William L. Moran, *The Amarna Letters* (Baltimore: Johns Hopkins Univ. Press, 1992).

[2] See, for example, A. Caquot, M. Sznycer, A. Herdner, *Textes ougaritiques 1: Mythes et légendes,* Littératures anciennes du Proche-Orient (LAPO) 7 (Paris, 1974); Caquot, J.-M. de Tarragon and J.-L. Cunchillos, *Textes ougaritiques II: Textes religieux, rituels, correspondance,* LAPO 14 (Paris, 1989); D. Pardee, *Les textes rituels, 2 fascicules,* Ras Shamra-Ougarit (RSO) 12 (Paris, 2000).

[3] See Anson F. Rainey, "Unruly Elements in Late Bronze Canaanite Society," ed. D.P. Wright et al., *Pomegranates and Golden Bells: Studies in Biblical, Jewish, and Near Eastern Ritual, Law, and Literature in Honor of Jacob Milgrom* (Winona Lake, IN: Eisenbrauns, 1995, pp. 481-496.

[4] See André Lemaire, "Recherches actuelles sur les origines de l'ancien Israël," *Journal Asiatique* 270 (1982), pp. 5-24.

[5] Lemaire, "La Haute Mésopotamie et l'origine des Benê Jacob," *Vetus Testamentum* 34 (1984), pp. 95-101.

[6] The name of the "god of their father" (Genesis 31:42,53), possibly "Pahad" (often translated "fear") is apparently found in the proper name "Zelo-pahad," perhaps carried by one of the heads of this group. See Lemaire, "Les Benê Jacob: Essai d'interprétation historique d'une tradition patriarcale," *Revue Biblique* 85, 1978, pp. 321-337.

[7] About these appellations, see T.J. Lewis, "The Identity and Function of El/Baal Berith," *Journal of Biblical Literature* 115, 1996, pp. 401-423. See also Lawrence E. Stager, "The Shechem Temple: Where Abimelech Massacred a Thousand," *Biblical Archaeology Review,* (*BAR*) July/August 2003.

[8] See Volkmar Fritz, "Die Bedeutung der vorpriesterschriftlichen Vätererzählungen für die Religionsgeschichte der Königszeit," in *Ein Gott allein? JHWH-Verehrung und biblischer Monotheismus im Kontext der israelitischen und altorientalischen Religionsgeschichte,* ed. W. Dietrich and M.A. Klopfenstein (Freiburg, 1994), pp. 403-411.

[9] See É. Dhorme, "Le nom du Dieu d'Israël," *Revue d'Histoire des Religions* 71/141 (1952), pp. 5-18.

[10] See J.A. Emerton, "The site of Salem, the city of Melchizedek (Genesis XIV 18)," in *Studies in the Pentateuch,* ed. Emerton, Supplements to Vetus Testamentum (SVT) 41 (Leiden, 1990), pp. 45-71

[11] See, for example, Emerton, "The Biblical High Place in the Light of Recent Study," *Palestine Exploration Quarterly* 129 (1997), pp. 116-132. Strangely enough A. Pagolu (*The Religion of the Patriarchs,* Journal for the Study of the Old Testament Supplement (JSOTS) 277 [Sheffield, 1998]) discusses the role played by the altar and the stela but seems to forget the sacred tree, mentioned in passing by M. Gleis (*Die Bamah,* Beihefte zur Zeitschrift für die Alttestamentliche Wissenschaft (BZAW) 251 [Berlin, 1997], p. 245), who does not recognize that the sacred tree is designated by the Hebrew word *asherah.*

[12] See Lemaire, "Cycle primitif d'Abraham et contexte géographico-historique," in *History and Traditions of Early Israel, Studies Presented to Eduard Nielsen,* eds. Lemaire and B. Otzen, SVT 50, (Leiden, 1993), pp. 62-75; "Vues nouvelles sur la tradition biblique d'Abraham," in *Les routes du Proche-Orient, Des séjours d'Abraham aux caravanes de l'encens,* ed. Lemaire (Paris, 2000), pp. 21-31. This dating is questioned, for example, by T.C. Römer in "Recherches actuelles sur le cycle d'Abraham," in *Studies in the Book of Genesis: Literature, Redaction and History,* ed. A. Wénin, Bibliotheca Ephemeridum Theologicarum Lovaniensium (BETL) 140 (Leuven, 2001), pp. 179-211; Römer, however, recognizes that the traditions about Abraham are geographically connected with Hebron or the region around Hebron (p. 189).

NOTES TO CHAPTER 2

[1] See Lemaire, "Notes d'épigraphie nord-ouest sémitique," *Syria* 64 (1987), pp. 295-316; "La stèle de Mésha et l'histoire de l'ancien Israël," in *Storia e tradizioni di Israele, Scritti in onore di J. Alberto Soggin,* ed. D. Garrone and F. Israel (Brescia, 1991), pp. 143-183.

[2] See Avraham Biran and Joseph Naveh, "The Tel Dan Inscription: A New Fragment," *Israel Exploration Journal (IEJ)* 45 (1995), pp. 1-18.

[3] Lemaire, "The Tel Dan Stela as a Piece of Royal Historiography," *Journal for the Study of the Old Testament* 81 (1998), pp. 3-14.

[4] See R.S. Hess, "The Divine Name Yahweh in Late Bronze Age Sources," *Ugarit-Forschungen* 23 (1991), pp. 181-188; *Amarna Personal Names,* American Schools of Oriental Research, Dissertation Series 9 (Winona Lake, IN: Eisenbrauns, 1993). For more on the absence of "YHWH" in Amorite onomastics, see M.P. Streck, "Der Gottesname 'Jahwe' und das amurritische Onomastikon," *Die Welt des Orients* 30 (1999), pp. 35-46.

[5] The hypothesis about the existence of Yahwistic but non-Israelite names rests upon a somewhat dubious philology; see K. Lawson Younger, "Yahweh at Ashkelon and Calah? Yahwistic Names in Neo-Assyrian," *Vetus Testamentum* 52 (2002), pp. 207-218.

[6] See, for example, L.E. Axelsson, *The Lord Rose Up from Seir,* Coniectanea Biblica Old Testament Series (CBOTS) 25 (Lund, 1987), pp. 48-55.

[7] See Lemaire, "D'Édom à l'Idumée et à Rome," in *Des Sumériens aux Romains d'Orient. La perception géographique du monde. Espaces et territoires au Proche-Orient ancien,* ed. A. Sérandour, Antiquités sémitiques 2 (Paris, 1997), pp. 81-103.

[8] J. Janssen, "Les monts Se'ir dans les textes égyptiens," *Biblica* 15 (1934), pp. 537-538; S. Ahituv, *Canaanite Toponyms in Ancient Egyptian Documents* (Leiden, 1984), p. 169

[9] R. Giveon, *Les Bédouins Shosou des documents égyptiens,* Documenta et Monumenta Orientis Antiqui (DMOA) 22 (Leiden, 1971), p. 132; K.A. Kitchen, "The Egyptian Evidence on Ancient Jordan," in *Early Edom and Moab. The Beginning of the Iron Age in Southern Jordan,* ed. P. Bienkowski, Sheffield Archaeological Monographs (SAM) 7 (Sheffield, 1992), pp. 21-34.

[10] See Lemaire, "Date et origine des inscriptions paléo-hébraïques et phéniciennes de Kuntillet 'Ajrud," *Studi epigrafici e linguistici* 1 (1984), pp. 131-144.

[11] See "Kuntillet 'Ajrud," in *The Anchor Bible Dictionary* IV, ed. D.N. Freedman (New York, 1992),

pp. 103-109.

12 See O. Eissfeldt, "Protektorat der Midianiter über ihre Nachbarn in letzten Viertel des 2. Jahrtausends v. Chr," *Journal of Biblical Literature* 87 (1968), pp. 383-393; Lemaire, "Les premiers rois araméens dans la tradition biblique," in *The World of the Aramaeans I, Biblical Studies in Honour of P.-E. Dion,* ed. P.M.M. Daviau *et al.*, JSOTS 324, (Sheffield, 2002), pp. 113-143.

13 See P. Parr, "Contacts between Northwest Arabia and Jordan in the Late Bronze and Iron Ages," in *Studies in the History and Archaeology of Jordan* I, ed. A. Hadidi (Amman, 1982), pp. 127-133; J.F.A. Sawyer and D.J.A. Clines eds., *Midian, Moab, and Edom, The History and Archaeology of Late Bronze and Iron Age Jordan and North-West Arabia,* JSOTS 24 (Sheffield, 1983); E.A. Knauf, *Midian: Untersuchungen zur Geschichte Palästinas und Nordarabiens am Ende des 2. Jahrtausends v. Chr.,* Abhandlungen des Deutschen Palästina-Vereins (ADPV) (Wiesbaden, 1988); V. Fritz, *Die Entstehung Israels im 12. und 11. Jahrhundert v. Chr.,* Biblische Enzyklopädie 2 (Stuttgart, 1996), pp. 175-177. See also the possible association with the copper mines in Timna and Feinan (Fritz, "Copper Mining and Smelting in the Area of Feinân at the end of Iron Age I," in *Aharon Kempinski Memorial Volume. Studies in Archaeology and Related Disciplines,* ed. Eliezer D. Oren and Shmuel Ahituv, Beer-Sheva 15 [Beer-Sheva, 2002], pp. 93-102).

14 See, for example, J. Leclant, "Fouilles et travaux en Égypte et au Soudan, 1961-1962," *Orientalia* 32 (1963), pp. 184-219; "Le 'tétragramme' à l'époque d'Aménophis III," in *Near Eastern Studies Dedicated to H.I.H. Prince Takahito Mikasa,* ed. M. Mori, Bulletin of the Middle Eastern Culture Center in Japan V (Wiesbaden, 1991), pp. 215-217.

15 See B. Grdseloff, "Édom d'après les sources égyptiennes," *Revue de l'Histoire Juive en Égypte* 1 (1947), pp. 69-99; Caquot, "Le nom du Dieu d'Israël," *Positions luthériennes* 14 (1966), pp. 244-257.

16 See E. Edel, "Die Ortsnamenlisten in den Tempeln von Aksha, Amarah und Soleb im Sudan," *Biblische Notizen* 11, 1980, pp. 63-79.

17 See Giveon, *Les Bédouins Shosou,* pp. 26-28, 74-77.

18 See Giveon, *Les Bédouins Shosou,* notes 16a, 25 and 38.

19 M. Görg, "Jahwe—ein Toponym?" Biblische Notizen 1 (1976), pp. 7-14; Knauf, *Midian,* pp. 46-48 (compare, for example, the mountain/god "Carmel," in Tacitus, *Histoires* 2.78.3); Görg, "YHWH—ein Toponym? Weitere Perspektiven," *Biblische Notizen* 101 (2000), pp. 10-14.

20 As "Aharonide" refers to priestly descendants of Aaron, "Elide" refers to priestly descendants of Eli (1 Samuel 1:3ff).

21 For an attempt to place these stories in an Egyptian context, see James K. Hoffmeier, *Israel in Egypt* (New York, 1997).

22 Roland de Vaux, *Histoire ancienne d'Israël, Des origines à l'installation en Canaan* (Paris, 1971), p. 311 (published in English as *The Early History of Israel,* trans. by David Smith [Philadelphia: Westminster, 1978]).

23 See D. Valbelle, "Le paysage historique de l'Exode," in *La protohistoire d'Israël, de l'exode à la monarchie,* ed. E.-M. Laperrousaz (Paris, 1990), pp. 87-107.

24 De Vaux, *Histoire ancienne d'Israël* (English ed., *The Early History of Israel*), p. 313. This Midianite interpretation was first broached in 1862 by F.W. Ghillany (also known as Richard von der Alm) and then independently by others; see, for example, L.E. Binns, "Midianite Elements in Hebrew Religions," *Journal of Theological Studies* 31, 1930, pp. 337-354; H.H. Rowley, *From Joseph to Joshua* (London, 1958), pp. 149-152; N.P. Lemche, "The Development of Israelite Religion in the Light of Recent Studies on the Early History of Israel," in *Congress Volume, Leuven 1989,* ed. J.A. Emerton, SVT 43 (Leiden, 1991), pp. 97-115; K. van der Toorn, *Family Religion in Babylonia, Syria and Israel,* Studies in the History and Culture of the Ancient Near East (SHCANE) 7 (Leiden, 1996), pp. 282-285; N. Shupak, "The God from Teman and the Egyptian Sun God: A Reconsideration of Habakuk 3:3-7," *Journal of the Ancient Near Eastern Society*

28, (2002), pp. 97-116; Ch. Frevel, "'Jetzt habe ich erkannt, dass YHWH grösser ist als alle Götter': Ex 18 und seine kompositionsgeschichtliche Stellung im Pentateuch," *Biblische Zeitschrift* 47 (2003), pp. 3-22.

[25] In verse 12, the mention of the holocaust and Aaron could have been added by a later priestly editor. See A. Cody, Exodus 18:12 Jethro Accepts a Covenant with the Israelites," *Biblica* 49 (1968), pp. 153-166.

[26] See de Vaux, *Histoire ancienne d'Israël* (English ed., *The Early History of Israel*), p. 433: "ce n'est pas le monothéisme."

NOTES TO CHAPTER 3

[1] See K.A. Kitchen, "The Egyptian Evidence on Ancient Jordan," in *Early Edom and Moab: The Beginning of the Iron Age in Southern Jordan,* ed. P. Bienkowski, SAM 7 (Sheffield, 1992), pp. 21-34; D. Warburton, "Egyptian Campaigns in Jordan Revisited," *Studies in the History and Archaeology of Jordan* VII (Amman, 2001), pp. 233-237.

[2] The dating of this collection is uncertain, because all that remains of the collection is the passage quoted in Numbers 21:14 (and perhaps 21:17-18); the phrase "YHWH wars" appears again only in reference to David (1 Samuel 18:17, 25:28).

[3] See de Vaux, *Histoire ancienne d'Israël* (English ed., *The Early History of Israel*), p. 579.

[4] See Lemaire, "Aux origines d'Israël: la montagne d'Ephraïm et le territoire de Manassé," in *La protohistoire d'Israël*, ed. Laperrousaz (1990), pp. 183-292.

[5] See, with bibliography, A.F. Rainey, "Israel in Merneptah's Inscriptions and Reliefs," *IEJ* 51 (2001), pp. 57-75; B. Lurson, "Israël sous Merenptah ou le sort de l'ennemi dans l'Égypte ancienne," in *Étrangers et exclus dans le monde biblique. Colloque international à l'Université Catholique de l'Ouest, Angers, les 21 et 22 février 2002,* ed. J. Riaud (Angers, 2003), pp. 45-62.

[6] See T.N.D. Mettinger, "YHWH SABAOTH—The Heavenly King on the Cherubin Throne," in *Studies in the Period of David and Solomon and Other Essays,* ed. T. Ishida (Tokyo, 1982), pp. 109-138; S.-M. Kang, *Divine War in the Old Testament and in the Ancient Near East,* BZAW 177 (Berlin, 1989), pp. 198-201. The phrase "YHWH Zebaot" is attested in a Judahite eighth-century B.C.E. inscription probably from Khirbet el-Qom (see Naveh, "Hebrew Graffiti from the First Temple Period", *IEJ* 51 [2001], pp. 194-207).

[7] See Lemaire, "Aux origines d'Israël," pp. 242-246.

[8] See Genesis 32:28: "You shall no longer be called Jacob, but Israel."

[9] See Lemaire, "Le décalogue: essai d'histoire de la rédaction," in *Mélanges bibliques et orientaux en l'honneur de M. Henri Cazelles,* ed. Caquot and M. Delcor, Alter Orient und Altes Testament (AOAT) 212 (Neukirchen, 1981), pp. 259-295.

[10] See A. Mazar, "The 'Bull Site,' an Iron Age I Open Cult Place," *Bulletin of the American Schools of Oriental Research* 247 (1982), pp. 27-42; and "Bronze Bull Found in Israelite 'High Place' from the Time of Judges," *BAR,* September/October 1983.

[11] See Adam Zertal, "An Early Iron Age Cultic Site on Mount Ebal: Excavation Seasons 1982-1987," *Tel Aviv* 13-14 (1986-1987), pp. 105-164; "Has Joshua's Altar Been Found on Mt. Ebal?" *BAR,* January/February 1985; and Aharon Kempinski, "Joshua's Altar—An Iron Age I Watchtower," *BAR,* January/February 1986. The recent discovery of a rock-cut altar near Shiloh is difficult to date: see Yoel Elitzur and Doron Nir-Zevi, "A Rock-Hewn Altar Near Shiloh," *Palestine Exploration Quarterly* 135 (2003), pp. 30-36. See also Elitzur and Nir-Zevi, "Four-Horned Altar Discovered in Judean Hills," *BAR,* May/June 2004.

[12] See Lemaire, "Aux origines d'Israël," pp. 284-286.

[13] See Israel Finkelstein, *The Archaeology of the Israelite Settlement* (Jerusalem, 1988), p. 201.

NOTES TO CHAPTER 4

[1] See I. Singer, "Towards the Image of Dagon, the God of the Philistines," *Syria* 69 (1992), pp. 431-450.

[2] See Caquot and Ph. de Robert, *Les livres de Samuel,* Commentaire de l'Ancien Testament VI (Geneva, 1994), p. 20.

[3] Baruch Halpern, *David's Secret Demons: Messiah, Murderer, Traitor, King,* (Grand Rapids, MI: Eerdmans 2001).

[4] See Jon D. Levenson and Halpern, "The Political Import of David's Marriages," *Journal of Biblical Literature* 99 (1980), pp. 507-518.

[5] See, generally, *Divine War,* pp. 193-224; A. van der Lingen, *Les guerres de Yahvé,* Lectio divina 139 (Paris, 1990).

[6] See Lemaire, "La montagne de Juda," in *La protohistoire d'Israël, de l'exode à la monarchie,* ed. Laperrousaz (Paris, 1990), pp. 293-298.

[7] See Lemaire, "Cycle primitif d'Abraham et contexte géographico-historique," in *History and Traditions of Early Israel, Studies Presented to Eduard Nielsen,* ed. A. Lemaire and B. Otzen., SVT 50 (Leiden, 1993), pp. 62-75.

[8] See, for example, Eissfeldt, "El and Yahweh," *Journal of Semitic Studies* 1 (1956), pp. 25-37; and J. Day, *Yahweh and the Gods and Goddesses of Canaan,* JSOTS 265 (Sheffield, 2000), pp. 13-34.

[9] De Vaux, *Histoire ancienne d'Israël,* p. 428.

[10] See, for example, M.S. Smith, *The Early History of God, Yahweh and the Other Deities in Ancient Israel* (New York, 1990: pp. 161-168; and Grand Rapids, 2002: pp. 182-191).

[11] See Emerton, "Some problems in Genesis XIV," in *Studies in the Pentateuch,* ed. Emerton, SVT 41 (Leiden, 1990), pp. 73-102.

[12] See Lemaire and Durand, *Les inscriptions araméennes,* pp. 113, 120-121.

[13] See F. Bron, *Recherches sur les inscriptions phéniciennes de Karatepe,* Hautes Études Orientales (HEO) 11 (Geneva, 1979), pp. 14, 25, 120. The complete formula, "Baal of the heavens and El creator of the earth," evokes even more precisely the formula used by Melchisedek.

[14] See Nahman Avigad, "Excavations in the Jewish Quarter of the Old City of Jerusalem, 1971," *IEJ* 22 (1972), pp. 193-200; see also Patrick D. Miller, *Israelite Religion and Biblical Theology: Collected Essays,* JSOTS 267 (Sheffield, 2000), pp. 45-50.

[15] Just as there are parallels between Abraham and David, there are parallels between Melchisedek and Zadok, the priest of Jerusalem whom David takes into his service beside Abiathar.

[16] See, for example, J. Day, "Yahweh and the Gods and Goddesses of Canaan," in *Ein Gott allein?* ed. Dietrich and Klopfenstein, pp. 181-196.

[17] See H. Niehr, *Der höchste Gott: Alttestamentlicher JHWH-Glaube in Kontext syrisch-kanaanischer Religion des 1. Jahrtausend v. Chr.,* BZAW 190 (Berlin, 1990); and "The Rise of YHWH in Judahite and Israelite Religion. Méthodological and Religio-Historical Aspects," in *The Triumph of Elohim. From Yahwisms to Judaisms,* ed. D.V. Edelman (Kampen, 1995), pp. 45-72.

[18] The role of the second name, "Yedidiah," given to Solomon according to Nathan's oracle, is not clear. It could have been a kind of nickname rather than a true name, unless it was a name given by David/Nathan in addition to the one given by Bathsheba.

[19] For a possible confusion šēlōšîm/šālîšîm, see. N. Na'aman, "The List of David's Officers (šālîšîm)," *Vetus Testamentum* 38 (1988), pp. 71-79.

[20] Laperrousaz, "A-t-on dégagé l'angle sud-est du 'temple de Salomon'?" *Syria* 50 (1973), pp. 355-399; and *Les temples de Jérusalem* (Paris, 1999), pp. 33-43.

[21] These two aspects will be found again in the temples of Dan and Bethel established by Jeroboam I (1 Kings 12:26-33; compare Amos 7:13) and in the temple of Samaria.

NOTES TO CHAPTER 5

[1] See, for example, Moshe Weinfeld, *Deuteronomy 1-11,* The Anchor Bible Dictionary 5 (New York, 1991), p. 338: "Deut. 6:4 is a kind of liturgical confessional proclamation and by itself cannot be seen as monotheistic."

[2] See, for example, Innocent Himbaza, "Dt 32,8, une correction tardive des scribes, Essai d'interpretation et de datation," *Biblica* 83 (2002), pp. 527-548.

[3] See, for example, P. Buis, *La notion d'alliance dans l'Ancien Testament,* Lectio divina 88 (Paris, 1976).

[4] See, for example, "You shall worship no other god, because YHWH, whose name is Jealous, is a jealous God" (Exodus 34:14).

[5] See Lemaire, "Essai sur les religions ammonite, moabite et édomite (X-VIe s. av. n. è.)," *Revue de la Société Ernest-Renan* NS 41 (1993), pp. 41-67; and "Déesses et dieux de Syrie-Palestine d'après les inscriptions (c. 1000-500 av. n. è.)," in *Ein Gott allein?,* ed. Dietrich and Klopfenstein, pp. 127-158.

[6] Lemaire, "Déesses et dieux de Syrie-Palestine d'après les inscriptions (c. 1000-500 av. n. è.)," in *Ein Gott allein?,* ed. Dietrich and Klopfenstein, pp. 127-158.

[7] For the justification of this reading and interprétation, see Lemaire, "Notes d'épigraphie nord-ouest sémitique," *Syria* 64 (1987), pp. 205-216. The reading proposed by A. Schade, "New Photographs Supporting the Reading *ryt* in Line 12 of the Mesha Inscription," *IEJ* 55 (2005), pp. 205-208 is contradicted by a new examination of the stela and of the squeeze: see Lemaire, "New Photographs and *ryt* or *hyt* in Mesha, Line 12," to be published in *IEJ.*

[8] See Avigad and Benjamin Sass, *Corpus of West Semitic Stamp Seals,* (Jerusalem, 1997), pp. 372-386; and Robert Deutsch and Michael Heltzer, *Windows to the Past,* (Tel Aviv-Jaffa, 1997), pp. 59-61.

[9] This epigraphic evidence is enough to reject B. Lang's hypothesis of a "Yahweh-alone movement" that appeared around 750 B.C.E. (see *The Hebrew God: Portrait of an Ancient Deity* [New Haven, 2002], p. 188).

NOTES TO CHAPTER 6

[1] The god "Baal," whose name etymologically means "Master," was known in 13th-century B.C.E. Ugarit and in the Phoenician/Punic world during the first millennium B.C.E. He was presented as a young storm god, and he seems to have been the most prominent god in the pantheons of numerous Levantine cities, especially Tyre.

[2] Josephus, *Against Apion* 1.123.

[3] "Baalist" designates here a theophoric name containing the divine name "Baal."

[4] See Lemaire, *Les inscriptions hébraïques I. Les ostraca,* LAPO 9 (Paris, 1977), p. 55.

[5] See Lemaire, "Joas, roï d'Israël, et la première rédaction du cycle d'Élisée," in *Pentateuchal and Deuteronomistic Studies,* ed. C. Breckelmans and J. Lust, BETL 94 (Leuven 1990), pp. 245-254. In any case, the emphasis on the Yahwist sanctuary on Mount Carmel is clearly pre-Deuteronomistic.

[6] See Lemaire, "Asher et le royaume de Tyr," in *Phoenicia and the Bible,* ed. E. Lipinski, Studia Phoenicia XI (Leuven, 1991), pp. 131-150.

[7] See M. Masson, "Rois et prophètes dans le cycle d'Élie," in *Prophètes et rois, Bible et Proche-Orient,* ed. Lemaire (Paris, 2001), pp. 119-131.

[8] See, for example, L.K. Handy, *Among the Host of Heaven* (Winona Lake, 1994); "The Appearance of Pantheon in Judah," in *The Triumph of Elohim,* ed. D.V. Edelman, Contributions to Biblical Exegesis and Theology (CBET) 13 (Kampen, 1995), pp. 27-43; and B. Lang, "Monotheismus," in *Neues Bibel-Lexikon* 10, ed. M. Görg and B. Lang (Soloturn/Düsseldorf, 1995), col. 834-844 (in col. 835, however, Lang bases his argument on the Deir 'Alla inscriptions that are in Aramaic, not Hebrew).

[9] See, for example, C. Frevel, *Aschera und der Ausschliesslichkeitsanspruch YHWHs,* Bonner Biblische Beiträge (BBB) 94/1-2 (Weinheim, 1995); and H. Niehr, "Religio-Historical Aspects of the 'Early Post-Exilic' Period," in *The Crisis of Israelite Religion, Transformation of Religious Tradition in Exilic and Post-Exilic Times,* ed. B. Becking and M.C.A. Korpel, Oudtestamentische Studien (OTS) 42 (Leiden, 1999), pp. 228-244.

NOTES TO CHAPTER 7

[1] Lemaire, "Les inscriptions de Khirbet el-Qôm et l'ashérah de YHWH," *Revue biblique* 84 (1977), pp. 595-608.

[2] See Zev Meshel, *Kuntillet 'Ajrud: A Religious Centre from the Time of the Judaean Monarchy on the Border of Sinai,* Cat. no. 175 (Jerusalem, 1978). See also Meshel, "Did Yahweh Have a Consort?" *BAR,* March/April 1979.

[3] S.A. Wiggins, "Asherah Again: Binger's Asherah and the State of Asherah Studies," *Journal of Northwest Semitic Languages* 24 (1998), pp. 231-240.

[4] According to a religious concept well attested in Phoenicia, the pantheon of each city was headed by a divine couple consisting of a great god and a great goddess (see Lemaire, "Déesses et dieux de Syrie-Palestine d'après les inscriptions [c. 1000 - 500 av. n. è.]," in *Ein Gott allein?* ed. Dietrich and Klopfenstein, pp. 127-158. Those who argue that Asherah is a goddess say that the same situation held in Israel and Judah: YHWH was the great god and Asherah was the great goddess (see Meshel, "Did Yahweh Have a Consort?").

[5] See Moran, *The Amarna Letters,* nos. 60-149, 362, 367.

[6] For this dating, see S. Dalix, "Suppiluliuma (II?) dans un texte alphabétique d'Ugarit et la date d'apparition de l'alphabet cunéiforme. Nouvelle proposition de datation des "Archives Ouest"." *Semitica* 48 (1999), pp. 5-15.

[7] See J. Freu, "La fin d'Ugarit et de l'Empire hittite. Données nouvelles et chronologie," *Semitica* 48 (1999), pp. 17-39; and Singer, "A Political History of Ugarit," *Handbook of Ugaritic Studies,* ed. G.E. Watson and N. Wyatt, HdO 1.39 (Leiden, 1999), pp. 603-733.

[8] See Pardee, *Les textes rituels* II, RSO XII (Paris, 2000), p. 1,118.

[9] Taking into account a few texts in which the word is restored so as to be practically certain, see J.-L. Cunchillos and J.-P. Vita, *Concordancia de Palabras Ugariticas en morfologia desplegada* (Madrid-Zaragoza, 1995), pp. 169-171.

[10] Cf., for example, L.K. Handy, *Among the Host of Heaven: The Syro-Palestinian Pantheon as Bureaucracy,* 1994, pp. 65-95.

[11] See J. Hoftijzer and K. Jongeling, *Dictionary of the North-West Semitic Inscriptions* I (Leiden, 1995), p. 129.

[12] See, for example, Seymour Gitin, "Seventh Century B.C.E. Cultic Elements at Ekron," in *Biblical Archaeology Today, 1990, Proceedings of the Second International Congress on Biblical Archaeology Jerusalem, June-July 1990,* ed. Biran and Joseph Aviram (Jerusalem, 1993), pp. 248-258.

[13] See Lemaire, "Phénicien et philistin: paléographie et dialectologie," in *Actas del IV congreso internacional de estudios fenicios y punicos, Cadiz, 2 al 6 de Octubre de 1995,* ed. M.E. and Aubet and M. Barthélemy (Cadix, 2000, pp. 243-249).

[14] F. Bron, "Notes sur le culte d'Athirat en Arabie du Sud préislamique," in *Études sémitiques et samaritaines offertes à Jean Margain,* ed. Ch.-B. Amphoux *et al.* (Lausanne, 1998), pp. 75-79).

[15] See D.A. Dorsey, "The Location of the Biblical Makkedah," *Tel Aviv* 7 (1980), pp. 185-193.

[16] William G. Dever, "Iron Age Epigraphic Material from the Area of Khirbet el-Kôm," *Hebrew Union College Annual* 40-41 (1969-1970), pp. 139-204.

[17] Lemaire, "Les inscriptions de Khirbet el-Qôm et l'*ashérah* de Yhwh," *Revue Biblique* 84 (1977),

pp. 595-608.

[18] See J.M. Hadley, "The Khirbet el-Qom Inscription," *Vetus Testamentum* 37 (1987), pp. 50-62; *The Cult of Asherah in Ancient Israel and Judah* (Cambridge, 2000), pp. 84-102, 207; and J. Renz, *Die althebräischen Inschriften,* Handbuch der althebräischen Epigraphik 1.1 (Darmstadt, 1995), pp. 202-211 (but the inscription is to be dated to the middle of the eighth century B.C.E rather than to the last quarter of the eighth century).

[19] See Lemaire, "Date et origine des inscriptions hébraïques et phéniciennes de Kuntillet 'Ajrud," *Studi epigrafici e linguistici* 1 (1984), pp. 131-143.

[20] See Meshel, "Kuntillet 'Ajrud," in *The Anchor Bible Dictionary* IV, ed. David Noel Freedman (New York, 1992), pp. 103-109.

[21] See J.M. Hadley, *The Cult of Asherah in Ancient Israel and Judah* (Cambridge, 2000); and B.B. Schmidt, "The Iron Age pithoi Drawings from Horvat Teman or Kuntillet 'Ajrud: Some New Proposals," *Journal of Ancient Near Eastern Religions* 2 (2003), pp. 91-125.

[22] See M. Heide, "Die theophoren Personennamen der Kuntillet-'Ajrûd Inscriften," *Die Welt des Orients* 32 (2002, pp. 110-120).

[23] This argument has been given new emphasis by Emerton, "'Yahweh and his Asherah': the goddess or her symbol?" *Vetus Testamentum* 49 (1999), pp. 315-338. See also Day, *Yahweh and the Gods and Goddesses of Canaan,* JSOTS 265 (Sheffield, 2000), p. 51.

[24] For a discussion of the sacred tree or thicket in Palestinian pagan sanctuaries through the first century C.E., see J.-M. Nieto Ibanez, "The Sacred Grove of Scythopolis (Flavius Josephus *Jewish War* II 466-471)," *IEJ* 49 (1999), pp. 260-268.

[25] Compare *nt'*: Deuteronomy 16:21.

[26] Compare *ntš*: Micah 5:3.

[27] Compare *krt*: Exodus 34:13; Judges 6:25-30 and 2 Kings 18:4, 23:14.

[28] Compare *gd'*: Deuteronomy 7:5; 2 Chronicles 14:2.

[29] Compare *ktt*: 2 Chroniques 34:7; and *šbr*: 2 Chronicles 34:4.

[30] Compare *śrp*: Deuteronomy 12:3; 2 Kings 23:15, 31:1. Compare also *b'r*: 2 Chronicles 19:3.

[31] Compare *'md*: 2 Kings 13:6 and 2 Chronicles 33:19; compare also *qwm*: Isaiah 27:9 and 2 Chronicles 33:3.

[32] Some commentators interpret the *asherah* as a wooden symbol or statue of the goddess Asherah. However, the actions that can be performed on the *asherah* are more consistent with a tree than with a wooden symbol or statue, for which one would have expected such actions as carving.

[33] See A.E. Cowley, *Aramaic Papyri of the Fifth Century B.C.* (Oxford, 1923), no. 44:3; 71:20; P. Grelot, *Documents araméens d'Égypte,* LAPO 5 (Paris, 1972), pp. 95-96; J. Teixidor, *The Pagan God, Popular Religion in the Greco-Roman Near East* (Princeton, 1977), pp. 31, 86-87; and van der Toorn "Herem-Bethel and Elephantine Oath Procedure," *Zeitschrift für die alttestamentliche Wissenschaft* 98 (1986), pp. 282-284.

[34] See Jeffrey H. Tigay, "A Second Temple Parallel to the Blessings from Kuntillet 'Ajrud," *IEJ* 40 (1990), p. 218.

[35] See Teixidor, *The Pagan God,* p. 87; L. Nehmé, "Une inscription inédite de Bosra (Syrie)," in *Études sémitiques et samaritaines offertes à Jean Margain,* ed. Ch.-B. Amphoux *et al.* (Lausanne, 1998), pp. 62-73.

[36] See Matthew 23:16-22.

[37] See W. Baudissin, *Studien zur semitischen Religionsgeschichte* (Leipzig, 1878, pp. 184-230); W.R. Smith, *Lectures on the Religion of the Semites* (London, 1894), p. 186; and M.J. Lagrange, *Études sur les religions sémitiques,* Études bibliques (Paris, 1905), pp. 169-180.

[38] This late dating is recognized by Hadley, "Yahweh and 'His Asherah': Archaeological and Tex-

tual Evidence for the Cult of the Goddess," in *Ein Gott allein?* ed. Dietrich and Klopfenstein, pp. 235-268.

[39] Raz Kletter, "Between Archaeology and Theology: The Pillar Figurines from Judah and the Asherah," in *Studies in the Archaeology of the Iron Age in Israel and Jordan,* ed. Amihai Mazar, JSOTS 331 (Sheffield, 2001), pp. 179-216.

[40] Kletter, "Between Archaeology and Theology," p. 205.

[41] Kletter, "Between Archaeology and Theology," p. 199.

[42] See Othmar Keel, *Goddesses and Trees, New Moon and Yahweh, Ancient Near Eastern Art and the Hebrew Bible,* JSOTS 261 (Sheffield, 1998), p. 38.

[43] P. Merlo, "Note critiche su alcune presunte iconografie della dea Ashera," *Studi epigrafici e linguistici* 14 (1997), pp. 43-64. S.A. Wiggins ("Of Asherahs and Trees: Some Methodological Questions," *Journal of Ancient Near Eastern Religions* 1 [2002], pp. 158-187) doubts the association of the goddess Asherah with a tree but he does not distinguish clearly enough between the Hebrew common name *asherah* and the proper name of the deity, Asherah.

NOTES TO CHAPTER 8

[1] See Lemaire, "Le Décalogue: essai d'histoire de la rédaction," in *Mélanges bibliques,* ed. Caquot and Delcor, pp. 259-295.

[2] The Cherubim mentioned in this description are clearly not representations of the deity; they are mythic beings playing the role of protectors of the deity in his sanctuary. At the most, in the tradition of empty thrones, they can be considered as a kind of pedestal for the deity.

[3] See P. Lecoq, *Les inscriptions de la Perse achéménide* (Paris, 1997), p. 184.

[4] See, for example, C. Uehlinger, "Eine anthropomorphe Kultstatue des Gottes von Dan?" *Biblische Notizen* 72 (1994), pp. 85-100.

[5] Uehlinger, "Anthropomorphic Cult Statuary in Iron Age Palestine and the Search for Yahweh's Cult Images," in *The Image and the Book. Iconic Cults, Aniconism, and the Rise of Book Religion in Israel and the Ancient Near East,* ed. van der Toorn (Leuven, 1997), pp. 97-155; "Israelite Aniconism in Context," *Biblica* 77 (1996), pp. 540-549; "'... und wo sind die Götter von Samarien?' Die Wegführung syrisch-palästinischer Kultstatuen auf einem Relief Sargons II in Ḥorsâbâd/Dûr-Sharrukîn," in *Und Mose schrieb dieses Lied auf,* ed. M. Dietrich et al., AOAT 250 (Münster, 1998), pp. 739-776; H. Niehr, "In search of YHWH's Cult Statue in the First Temple," in *The Image and the Book,* ed. van der Toorn, pp. 73-95; B. Becking, "Assyrian Evidence for Iconic Polytheism in Ancient Israel?" in *The Image and the Book,* ed. van der Toorn, pp. 157-171; and Lewis, "Divine Images and Aniconism in Ancient Israel," *Journal of the American Oriental Society* 118 (1998), pp. 42-47.

[6] Na'aman, "No Anthropomorphic Graven Image. Notes on the Assumed Anthropomorphic Cult Statues in the Temples of YHWH in the Pre-Exilic Period," *Ugarit-Forschungen* 31 (1999), pp. 391-415.

[7] See de Vaux, *Bible et Orient* (Paris, 1967), p. 155.

[8] See, for example, Frank Moore Cross, *Canaanite Myth and Hebrew Epic. Essays in the History of the Religion of Israel* (Cambridge, MA: 1973), p. 69.

[9] T.N.D. Mettinger, "Aniconism—a West Semitic Context for the Israelite Phenomenon," in *Ein Gott allein?* ed. Dietrich and Klopfenstein, pp. 159-178; *No Graven Image? Israelite Aniconism in Its Near Eastern Context,* CBOTS 42 (Stockholm, 1995); "The Roots of Aniconism: An Israelite Phenomenon in Comparative Perspective," in *Congress Volume, Cambridge 1995,* ed. Emerton, SVT 66 (Leiden, 1997), pp. 219-234; O. Loretz, "Semitischer Anikonismus und biblisches Bildverbot," *Ugarit-Forschungen* 26 (1994), pp. 209-223; and T.J. Lewis, "Divine Images and Ani-

conism in Ancient Israel?" *Journal of the American Oriental Society* 118 (1998), pp. 36-53. See also S.A. Fransouzoff, "A Parallel to the Second Commandment in the Inscriptions of Raybûn," *Proceedings of the Seminar for Arabian Studies* 28 (1998), pp. 61-67.

[10] See, for example, Durand, "Le culte des bétyles en Syria," in *Miscellanea Babylonica, Mélanges offerts à Maurice Birot,* ed. Durand and J.R. Kupper (Paris, 1985), pp. 79-84; "Assyriologie," *Annuaire du Collège de France* 102 (2002-2003), pp. 747-767; *Le culte des pierres et les monuments comménoratifs en Syrie amornite,* Mémoires de N.A.B.U 9 (Paris: 2005).

[11] See Mettinger, *No Graven Image?* pp. 84-90.

[12] See Mettinger, *No Graven Image?* pp. 57-68; and J.-F. Healey, *The Religion of the Nabataeans* (Leiden, 2001), pp. 185-188.

[13] See Delcor, "Les trônes d'Astarté," in *Atti del I Congresso internazionale di studi fenici e punici, Roma, 5-10 novembre 1979,* III (Rome, 1983), pp. 777-787; and Mettinger, *No Graven Image?* pp. 100-106.

[14] Mettinger, *No Graven Image?* p. 101.

[15] See U. Avner, "Ancient Cult Sites in the Negev and Sinai Deserts," *Tel Aviv* 11 (1984), pp. 115-131; "*Mazzebot* Sites in the Negev and Sinai and their Significance," in *Biblical Archaeology Today* (1990), ed. Biran and Aviram (Jerusalem), pp. 166-181; and Mettinger, *No Graven Image?* pp. 168-174.

[16] Mettinger, *No Graven Image?* pp. 57-68.

NOTES TO CHAPTER 9

[1] E. Renan, *Histoire du peuple d'Israël* II (Paris, 1889), p. 273.

[2] C. Clermont-Ganneau, *La stèle de Dhiban ou stèle de Mésa, roi de Moab* (Paris, 1870), pp. 5-8, 31.

[3] See G. Smith, "Addresses of Encouragements to Esarharhaddon," in *The Cuneiform Inscriptions of Western Asia* IV, ed. H.C. Rawlinson ed. (London, 1875, 1891), no. 68.

[4] See Lemaire, ed., *Prophètes et rois. Bible et Proche-Orient* (Paris, 2001).

[5] See Durand, "Les prophéties des textes de Mari," in *Oracles et prophéties dans l'Antiquité. Actes du colloque de Strasbourg 15-17 juin 1995,* ed. J.-G. Heintz, Travaux du centre de Recherche sur le Proche-Orient et la Grèce Antiques (TCRPOGA) (Paris, 1997), pp. 115-134.

[6] D. Charpin, "Prophètes et rois dans le Proche-Orient amorrite," in *Prophètes et rois,* ed. Lemaire, pp. 21-53.

[7] See Durand, "Le mythologème du combat entre le dieu de l'orage et la mer en Mésopotamie," *MARI* 7 (1993), pp. 41-61.

[8] Lemaire, ed., *Prophètes et rois,* pp. 13-14.

[9] See S. Parpola, *Assyrian Prophecies,* SAA 9 (Helsinki, 1997); M. Nissinen, *References to Prophecy in Neo-Assyrian Sources,* SAAS 7 (Helsinki, 1998); Nissinen, ed., *Prophecy in its Ancient Near Eastern Context,* SBL Symposium Series 13 (Atlanta, 2000); P. Villard, "Les prophéties à l'époque néo-assyrienne," in *Prophètes et rois,* ed. Lemaire, pp. 55-84; and M. Weippert, "'König, fürchte dich nicht!' Assyrische Prophetie im 7. Jahrhundert v. Chr.," *Orientalia* 71 (2002), pp. 1-54.

[10] Villard, in *Prophètes et rois,* ed. Lemaire, p. 60.

[11] Villard, in *Prophètes et rois,* ed. Lemaire, p. 70.

[12] Villard, in *Prophètes et rois,* ed. Lemaire, pp. 72-79.

[13] Lemaire, "Prophètes et rois dans les inscriptions ouest-sémitiques," in *Prophètes et rois,* ed. Lemaire, pp. 85-115.

[14] Lemaire, "Prophètes et rois dans les inscriptions ouest-sémitiques," in *Prophètes et rois,* ed. Lemaire, pp. 103-104; and "'House of David' Restored in Moabite Inscription," *BAR,* May/June 1994.

[15] Lemaire, "Prophètes et rois dans les inscriptions ouest-sémitiques," in *Prophètes et rois,* ed. Lemaire, pp. 97-98; and "Fragments from the Book of Balaam Found at Deir Alla," *BAR,* September/October 1985.

[16] A similar religious idea is present in the story about Absalom's exile, which would cut him off "from the heritage of God" (2 Samuel 14:16).

[17] Regarding the hospitality of the Arabs in this story, see Lemaire, "Achab, l'exil d'Élie et les Arabes." in *Prophètes et rois*, ed. Lemaire, pp. 133-144.

[18] Regarding the political interpretation of this prophetic oracle, see Lemaire, "Prophètes et rois dans les inscriptions ouest-sémitiques," in *Prophètes et rois*, ed. Lemaire, pp. 86-93.

[19] See Charpin, "Prophètes et rois dans le Proche-Orient amorrite," in *Prophètes et rois*, ed. Lemaire, pp. 21-53.

NOTES TO CHAPTER 10

[1] The phrase "high place" (Hebrew, *bâmâh*) designates a type of traditional sanctuary in the open sky, a sacred enclosure generally containing an altar, a stela and a sacred tree.

[2] The horns of the altars were the most sacred part of the altar (see 1 Kings 2:28), and such horns in cut stone are attested at Tel Dan (see Biran, *Biblical Dan* [Jerusalem, 1994], p. 165), as well as at Megiddo and Beersheba.

[3] See A. Schenker, "Le monothéisme israélite: une dieu qui transcende le monde et les dieux," *Biblica* 78 (1997), pp. 436-448.

[4] Regarding this passage and its historical interest, see. J.T. Willis, "The Authenticity and Meaning of Micah 5:9-14," *Zeitschrift für die alttestamentliche Wissenschaft* 81 (1969), pp. 353-368. For more on the dating of the passage, see B. Renaud, *La formation du livre de Michée,* Études bibliques (Paris, 1997), pp. 267-270; and *Michée, Sophonie, Nahum,* Sources bibliques (Paris, 1987), pp. 112-115.

[5] See, for example, Na'aman, "The Debated Historicity of Hezekiah's Reform in the Light of Historical and Archaeological Research," *Zeitschrift für die alttestamentliche Wissenschaft* 107, 1995, pp. 179-195; L.S. Fried, "The High Places (*Bâmôt*) and the Reforms of Hezekiah and Josiah," *Journal of the American Oriental Society* 122 (2002), pp. 437-465.

[6] See Andrew G. Vaughn, *Theology, History, and Archaeology in the Chronicler's Account of Hezekiah,* Archaeology and Biblical Studies 4 (Atlanta, 1999).

[7] See Weippert, "Die 'deuteronomistischen' Beurteilungen der Könige von Israel und Juda und das Problem der Redaktion der Königsbücher," *Biblica* 53 (1972), pp. 301-339; W.B. Barrick, "On the Removal of the 'High-Places' in 1-2 Kings," *Biblica* 55 (1974), pp. 257-259; Lemaire, "Vers l'histoire de la rédaction des Livres des Rois," *Zeitschrift für die alttestamentliche Wissenschaft* 98 (1986), pp. 221-236 (= "Toward a Redactional History of the Book of Kings," in G.N. Knoppers and J.G. McConville, eds., *Reconsidering Israel and Judah* [Winona Lake, 2000], pp. 446-461]; Halpern and D.S. Vanderhooft, "The Editions of Kings in the 7th-6th Centuries B.C.E.," *Hebrew Union College Annual* 62 (1991), pp. 179-244; W.B. Barrick, "On the Meaning of *béyt-ha/bâmôt* and *bâtéy-habbâmôt* and the Composition of the Kings History," *Journal of Biblical Literature* 115/4 (1996), pp. 621-642; E. Eynikel, *The Reform of King Josiah and the Composition of the Deuteronomistic History,* OTS 33 (Leiden, 1996);and A.F. Campbell and M.A. O'Brien, *Unfolding the Deuteronomistic History* (Minneapolis, 2000).

[8] The unifying of the Hebrew people around a Yahwism that absorbed local deities and cults.

[9] The story of the Nehushtan is therefore earlier than the late-eighth century B.C.E. Like the "golden calf," the Nehushtan could have been a "Canaanite" tradition justified by a story connected to Moses/Aaron (see K. Koenen, "Eherne Schlange und goldenes Kalb. Ein Vergleich der Überlieferungen," *Zeitschrift für die alttestamentliche Wissenschaft* 111 [1999], pp. 353-372).

[10] See Anson F. Rainey, "Hezekiah's Reform and the Altar at Beer-Sheba and Arad," in *Scripture and Other Artifacts,* ed. Mordecai D. Cogan *et al.* (Louisville, 1994), pp. 333-354.

[11] See Aharoni, "Excavations at Tel Beer-sheba, Preliminary Report of the Fifth and Sixth Seasons, 1973-1974," *Tel Aviv* 2 (1975), pp. 146-168.

[12] It may well have been located in an open-air sanctuary near the well.

[13] Ze'ev Herzog, "The Fortress Mound at Tel Arad: An Interim Report," *Tel Aviv* 29 (2002), pp. 3-109; see also, "The Date of the Temple at Arad: Reassessment of the Stratigraphy and the Implications for the History of Religion in Judah," in *Studies in the Archaeology of the Iron Age in Israel and Jordan,* ed. Mazar, JSOTS 331 (Sheffield, 2001), pp. 156-178.

[14] The same is probably true of the Lachish sanctuary (see David Ussishkin, "The Level V 'Sanctuary' and 'High Place' at Lachish," in *Saxa loquentur. Studien zur Archäologie Palästinas/Israel. Festschrift für V. Fritz,* ed. C.G. den Hertog *et al.,* AOAT 302 (Münster, 2003), pp. 205-211.

[15] Na'aman, "The Debated Historicity of Hezekiah's Reform," pp. 191-193.

[16] Aharoni, *Investigations at Lachish, The Sanctuary and the Residency (Lachish V)* (Tel Aviv, 1975), pp. 26-32.

[17] David Ussishkin, "The Level V 'Sanctuary' and 'High Place' at Lachish," in C.G. den Hertog *et al.,* eds., *Saxa loquentur* (Münster, 2003), pp. 205-211; *The Renewed Archaeological Excavations at Lachich (1973-1994)* (Tel Aviv, 2004) I, pp. 105-109.

[18] Ussishkin, *The Conquest of Lachish by Sennacherib* (Tel Aviv, 1982), p. 105.

[19] See Israel Finkelstein and N.A. Silberman, *David and Solomon* (New York, 2006), Appendix E, pp. 267-269.

[20] This phenomenon was emphasized by Renan, "Nouvelles considérations sur le caractère général des peuples sémitiques et en particulier sur leur tendance au monothéisme." *Journal Asiatique* (1859), p. 273.

[21] See also Jeremiah 2:28: "For you have as many gods as you have towns, O Judah."

[22] Since Hezekiah's and Josiah's reforms had similar characteristics, it is difficult to distinguish the corresponding levels of composition in Deuteronomy, as emphasized by Weinfeld: "As the book of Deuteronomy was discovered in the days of Josiah (622 B.C.E.) we must suppose that the main layout of the book existed long before that time—that is, at the time of Hezekiah. But we still do not know what belongs to later Josianic elaboration and what existed before" (*Deuteronomy 1-11,* The Anchor Bible 5 [New York, 1991], p. 51).

[23] As shown by de Vaux ("Le lieu que Yahvé a choisi pour y établir son nom," in *Das ferne und nahe Wort, Festschrift L. Rost,* ed. F. Mass, BZAW 105 [Berlin, 1967], pp. 219-228) and S.L. Richter (*The Deuteronomic History and the Name Theology,* BZAW 318 [Berlin, 2002]), this phrase probably corresponds to the Akkadian *shuma shakānu* to indicate the taking possession of a town by a victorious king.

[24] See, for example, O. Keel, "Warum im Jerusalemer Tempel kein anthropomorphes Kultbild gestanden haben dürfte," in *Homo Pictor,* ed. G. Boehm, Colloquium Rauricum Band 7 (Leipzig, 2001), pp. 244-282: "Die Polemik gegen allerhand figurative Kultobjekte (Stier, Schlange) hat schlussendlich auch zur Ablehnung der heiligen Steine und der Lade geführt." The elimination of the stelae is also emphasized by Mettinger (*No Graven Image?* p. 25).

[25] See the contemporaneous inscription from Khirbet Beit Lei invoking the "God of Jerusalem/'LHY YRŠLM" (see Lemaire, "Prières en temps de crise: les inscriptions de Khirbet Beit Lei," *Revue Biblique* 83 [1976], pp. 558-569; and J. Renz, *Die althebräischen Inschriften,* Handbuch der althebräischen Epigraphik I/1 [Darmstadt, 1995], pp. 245-246).

NOTES TO CHAPTER 11

[1] See William M. Schniedewind, "History and Interpretation. The Religion of Ahab and Manasseh in the Book of Kings," *The Catholic Biblical Quarterly* 55 (1993), pp. 649-661; P.S.F. van Keulen,

Manasseh Through the Eyes of the Deuteronomist: The Manasseh Account (2 Kings 21:1-18) and the Final Chapters of the Deuteronomistic History, OTS 28 (Leiden, 1996).

[2] In the Deuteronomist's account, Manasseh is responsible for the fall of Jerusalem. See E. Ben Zvi, "The Account of the Reign of Manasseh in II Kings 21:1-18 and the Redactional History of the Book of Kings," *Zeitschrift für die alttestamentliche Wissenschaft* 103 (1991), pp. 355-374; Schniedewind, "History and Interpretation," pp. 649-661; P.S.F. van Keulen, *Manasseh Through the Eyes of the Deuteronomists,* OTS 38 (Leiden, 1996); E. Eynikel, "The Portrait of Manasseh and the Deuteronomistic History," in *Deuteronomy and Deuteronomic Literature, Festschrift C.H.W. Breckelmans,* ed. M. Vervenne and J. Lust, BETL 133 (Leuven, 1997), pp. 233-261; and Halpern, "Why Manasseh is blamed for the Babylonian exile: the evolution of a biblical tradition," *Vetus Testamentum* 48 (1998), pp. 473-514.

[3] This seems to correspond to the one mentioned in 2 Kings 21:5.

[4] About the historicity of this reform, see N. Lohfink, "The Cult Reform of Josiah of Judah: 2 Kings 22-23 as a Source for the History of Israelite Religion," in *Ancient Israelite Religion. Essays in Honor of F.M. Cross,* ed. Miller *et al.* (Philadelphia, 1987), pp. 459-475; and Uehlinger, "Gab es eine joschianische Kultreform?" in *Jeremia und die "deuteronomistische Bewegung",* ed. W. Gross, BBB 98 (Weinheim, 1995), pp. 57-89.

[5] The importance of the solar cult for the worship of YHWH has been the subject of several studies. See, in particular, J.W. McKay, *Religion in Judah under the Assyrians 732-609 B.C.* (London, 1973), pp. 28-73, 97-124; "Further Light on the Horses and Chariot of the Sun in the Jerusalem Temple (2 Kings 23:11)," *Palestine Exploration Quarterly* 105 (1973), pp. 167-169; H.-P. Stähli, *Solare Element im Jahweglauben des Alten Testaments,* Orbis Biblicuset Orientalis (OBO) 66 (Fribourg/Göttingen, 1985); Keel, "Conceptions religieuses dominantes en Palestine/Israël entre 1750 et 900," in *Congress Volume, Paris 1992,* ed. Emerton, SVT 61 (Leiden, 1995), pp. 119-144; Keel and Uehlinger, "Jahwe und die Sonnengottheit von Jerusalem," in *Ein Gott allein?* pp. 269-306; and N. Shupak, "The God from Teman and the Egyptian Sun God: A Reconsideration of Habakuk 3:3-7," *Journal of the Ancient Near Eastern Society* 28 (2002), pp. 97-116.

[6] See, for example, Delcor, "Les cultes étrangers en Israël au moment de la réforme de Josias d'après 2R 23. Étude de religions sémitiques comparées," in *Mélanges bibliques,* ed. Caquot and Delcor, pp. 91-123.

[7] See Akkadian *kamānu.*

[8] See Akkadian *manzaltu.*

[9] See T. Ornan, "Ištar as Depicted on Finds From Israel," in *Studies of the Archaeology of the Iron Age in Israel and Jordan,* ed. Mazar, JSOTS 331 (Sheffield, 2001), pp. 235-256.

[10] See E. Lipiński, *The Aramaeans. Their Ancient History, Culture, Religion,* Orientalia Lovaniensia Analecta 100 (Leuven, 2000), pp. 607-626.

[11] See, for example, Lemaire and Durand, *Les inscriptions,* pp. 23-58; and Lemaire, *Nouvelles tablettes araméennes,* Hautes Études Orientales 34 (Geneva, 2001), p. 11.

[12] See Lemaire, "Coupe astrale inscrite et astronomie araméenne," in *Michael, Historical, Epigraphical and Biblical Studies in Honor of Prof. Michael Heltzer,* ed. Y. Avishur and Deutsch (Tel Aviv/Jaffa, 1999), pp. 195-211.

[13] See, for example, Uehlinger, "Bildquellen und 'Geschichte Israels': Grundsätzliche Überlegungen und Fallbeipsiele," in *Steine—Bilder—Texte,* ed. C. Hardmeier (Leipzig, 2001), pp. 25-77.

[14] See Delcor, "Les cultes étrangers," in *Mélanges bibliques,* ed. Caquot and Delcor, pp. 91-123.

[15] Its historicity is generally recognized. See, for example, Uehlinger, "Gab es eine joschijanische Kultreform? Plädoyer für ein begründetes Minimum," in *Jeremia und die "deuteronomische Bewegung",* ed. W. Gross, BBB 98 (Weinheim, 1995), pp. 57-89.

[16] See Tigay, *You Shall Have No Other Gods: Israelite Religion in the Light of Hebrew Inscriptions*, Harvard Semitic Studies (HSSt) 31 (Atlanta, 1986).

[17] Avigad and Sass, *Corpus of West Semitic Stamp Seals* (Jerusalem, 1997); see also Deutsch and Lemaire, *Biblical Period Personal Seals in the Shlomo Moussaieff Collection* (Tel Aviv, 2000).

[18] Deutsch, *Messages from the Past, Hebrew Bullae from the Time of Isaiah Through the Destruction of the First Temple* (Tel Aviv, 1999); and *Biblical Period Hebrew Bullae. The Josef Chaim Kaufman Collection* (Tel Aviv, 2003).

[19] Sociologists generally distinguish among three levels of religion, whether ancient or modern: official religion, local religion practiced in local sanctuaries, and family religion (see H.M. Niemann, *Herrschaft, Königtum und Staat: Skizzen zur soziokulturellen Entwicklung im monarchischen Israel*, FAT 6 [Tübingen, 1993], pp. 227-245). The centralization of the cult in Jerusalem and the proportion of Yahwist names around 600 B.C.E. suggest that Yahwism was not only an official religion but also penetrated to other levels of society. According to the prophetic writings, those who deviated from official Yahwism were as likely to be members of the elites (influenced by cults of foreign gods) as members of the peasantry (perhaps influenced by fertility cults).

NOTES TO CHAPTER 12

[1] See F. Joannès and Lemaire, "Trois tablettes cunéiformes à onomastique ouest-sémitique (collection Sh. Moussaïeff)," *Transeuphratène* 17 (1999), pp. 17-34.

[2] The god Sin is the "master/king of the gods of heavens and earth." See, for example, M.-J. Seux, *Hymnes et prières aux dieux de Babylonie et d'Assyrie*, LAPO 8 (Paris, 1976), pp. 521-522; F. d'Agostino, *Nabonedo, Adda Guppi, il deserto e il dio luna. Storia, ideologia e propaganda nella Babilonia del VI sec. A.C.* (Pisa, 1994); P.-A. Beaulieu, "The Sippar Cylinder of Nabonidus (2.123A)," in *The Context of Scripture II, Monumental Inscriptions from the Biblical World*, ed. W. Hallo (Leiden, 2000), pp. 310-14; H. Schaudig, *Die Inschriften Nabonids von Babylon und Kyros' des Grossen*, AOAT 256 (Münster, 2001).

[3] See A. Berlegung, *Die Theologie der Bilder. Das Kultbild in Mesopotamien und die alttestamentliche Bilderpolemik unter besonderer Berücksichtigung der Herstellung und Einweihung der Statuen*, OBO 162 (Fribourg, 1998).

[4] See C. Walker and M. Dick, *The Induction of the Cult Image in Ancient Mesopotamia. The Mesopotamian Mīs Pî Ritual*, State Archives of Assyria Literary Texts 1 (Helsinki, 2001).

[5] See Berlejung, *Die Theologie der Bilder*, pp. 315-411: "Die Polemik gegen Kultbilder im Alten Testament."

[6] See especially M. Albani, *Der eine Gott und die himmlischen Heerscharen. Zur Begrundung des Monotheismus bei Deuterojesaja im Horizont der Astralisierung des Gottesverständnis im Alten Orient*, ABG 1 (Leipzig, 2000).

[7] YHWH's support for Cyrus in Deutero-Isaiah corresponds to Marduk's support for Cyrus in dominating the Babylonian empire. See Lecoq, *Les inscriptions de la Perse achéménide*, pp. 181-185; M. Cogan, "Cyrus Cylinder," in *The Context of Scripture II, Monumental Inscriptions from the Biblical World*, ed. Hallo, pp. 314-316; and H. Schaudig, *Die Inschriften*, pp. 552-556. Both texts are variants of Persian propaganda in favor of Cyrus; see, for example, M. Weippert, "'Ich bin Jahwe'—'Ich bin Ishtar von Arbela' Deuterojesaja im Lichte der neuassyrischen Prophetie," in *Prophetie und Psalmen, Festschrift für K. Seybold*, ed. B. Huwyler et al. AOAT 280 (Münster, 2001), pp. 31-59.

[8] *Histories* 1.131. See also Strabo 15.3.13: "The Persians do not set up statues or altars to their gods."

[9] Lecoq, *Les inscriptions de la Perse achéménide*, p. 246 (see also pp. 217, 219, 229, 232, 241).

[10] P. Briant, *Histoire de l'empire perse. De Cyrus à Alexandre* (Paris, 1996), p. 105.

[11] See J. Kellens, *Essays on Zarathustra and Zoroastrianism* (Costa Mesa, 2000), pp. 25-30. See also Kellens, ed., *La religion iranienne à l'époque achéménide. Actes du Colloque de Liège 11 décembre 1987* (Gand, 1991); "Les Achéménides dans le contexte indo-iranien," in *Recherches récentes sur l'Empire achéménide,* ed. F. Boussac, Topoi—Orient, Occident, Supplément 1 (Lyon, 1997), pp. 287-295; and G. Ahn, "Schöpfergott und Monotheismus," in *"Und Mose schrieb dieses Lied auf." Studien zum Alten Testament und zum Alten Orient, Festschrift für O. Loretz,* ed. M. Dietrich and I. Kottsieper, AOAT 250 (Münster, 1998), pp. 15-26; J. Kellens, *La Quatrième Naissance de Zarathoustra* (Paris, 2006).

[12] For more on the historical interpretation of this oracle, see Lemaire, "Oracles, politique et littérature dans les royaumes araméens et transjordaniens (IXe-VIIIe s. av. n. è.)," in *Oracles et prophéties dans l'Antiquité,* ed. Heintz, pp. 171-193.

NOTES TO CHAPTER 14

[1] J. Day reminds us that this historical interpretation is not new; see "The Religion of Israel," in *Text in Context. Essays by Members of the Society for Old Testament Study,* ed. A.D.H. Mayes (Oxford, 2000), pp. 428-453: "Many scholars now accept Wellhausen's view that absolute monotheism was not attained till Deutero-Isaiah during the Exile, and its development was a gradual process in which the monolatrous challenge of Elijah, the work of the classical prophets, and the Deuteronomistic reform movement played significant roles." See also R.K. Gnuse, *No Other Gods. Emergent Monotheism in Israel,* JSOTS 241 (Sheffield, 1997), pp. 62-128; and "The Emergence of Monotheism in Ancient Israel: A Survey of Recent Scholarship," *Religion* 29 (1999), pp. 315-336.

[2] See, for example, Grelot, *Documents araméens d'Égypte;* Bezalel Porten and Ada Yardeni, *Textbook of Aramaic Documents from Ancient Egypt* I-IV (Jerusalem, 1986-1999).

[3] Grelot, *Documents araméens d'Égypte,* no. 87.

[4] Cowley, *Aramaic Papyri of the Fifth Century B.C.,* no. 44:1-3; and Grelot, *Documents araméens d'Égypte,* no. 10.

[5] About this use of *Herem* (taboo/inviolable object) in the oath formulas and as a divinity in the Aramaic onomasticon, see van der Toorn, "Herem-Bethel and Elephantine Oath Procedure," pp. 282-285.

[6] Cowley, *Aramaic Papyri of the Fifth Century B.C.,* no. 7:7-8; and Grelot, *Documents araméens d'Égypte,* no. 9.

[7] Thus the name "'Anat-Yaho" is influenced by Aramaic; see van der Toorn, "'Anat-Yahu, Some Other Deities, and the Jews of Elephantine," *Numen* 39 (1992), pp. 80-101.

[8] The Ezra mission is dated to the seventh year of Artaxerxes (Ezra 7:7) who has been identified sometimes as Artaxerxes I (464-424 B.C.E.) and sometimes as Artaxerxes II (404-359 B.C.E.), though the later date is more likely. See, for example, Lemaire, "La fin de la première période perse en Égypt et la chronologie judéenne vers 400 av. J.-C.," *Transeuphratène* 9 (1995), pp. 51-62.

[9] The alternative spellings YHWH (Yaweh?) and YHW (Yahō) are attested in the Kuntillet 'Ajrud inscriptions (first half of the eighth century B.C.E.).

[10] Cowley, *Aramaic Papyri of the Fifth Century B.C.,* nos. 38:3,5 (=Grelot, *Documents araméens d'Égypte,* no. 98) and 40:1 (=Grelot, *Documents araméens d'Égypte,* no. 16). About this phenomenon, see T.M. Bolin, "The Temple of YHW at Elephantine and Persian Religious Policy," in *The Triumph of Elohim. From Yahwisms to Judaisms,* ed. D.V. Edelman (Kampen, 1995), pp. 127-142; and P.-E. Dion, "La religion des papyrus d'Éléphantine: un reflet du Juda d'avant l'exil," in *Kein Land für sich allein. Studien zum Kulturkontakt in Kanaan, Israel/Palästina und Ebirnāri für M. Weippert,* ed. U. Hübner and E.A. Knauf, OBO 186 (Fribourg, 2003), pp. 243-254.

[11] Cowley, *Aramaic Papyri of the Fifth Century B.C.*, nos. 30:2,15,28, 31:27 (=Grelot, *Documents araméens d'Égypte*, no. 102).

[12] Cowley, *Aramaic Papyri of the Fifth Century B.C.*, no. 32:4 (=Grelot, *Documents araméens d'É-gypte*, no. 103).

[13] See, for example, H. Niehr, *Der höchste Gott, Alttestamentlicher JHWH-Glaube im Kontext syrisch-kanaanäischer Religion des 1. Jahrtausends v. Chr.*, BZAW 190 (Berlin, 1990), pp. 48-51.

[14] See T.M. Bolin, "The Temple of YHW at Elephantine," in *The Triumph of Elohim*, ed. Edelman, p. 38, n. 38. Niehr suggests that these Aramaic and Hebrew phrases refer to the "inclusive monotheism" of Ahuramazda.

[15] See Niehr, "JHWH und die Rolle des Baalshamem," in *Ein Gott allein?* ed. Dietrich and Klopfen-stein, pp. 307-326.

[16] See Lemaire, "Remarques sur certaines légendes monétaires ciliciennes (Ve-IVe s. av. J.-C.)," in *Mécanismes et innovations monétaires dans l'Anatolie achéménide. Numismatique et histoire. Actes de la Table Ronde Internationale d'Istanbul, 22-23 mai 1997*, ed. O. Casabonne (Paris, 2000), pp. 129-141. The appellation "Master of the heavens" is later interpreted as referring to a celestial world where, in some way, "angels" take the place of "gods"; see, for example, K. Koch, "Monotheismus und Angelologie," in *Ein Gott allein?* ed. Dietrich and Klopfenstein, pp. 565-581.

[17] See Yaakov Meshorer and S. Qedar, *Samarian Coinage* (Jerusalem, 1999), no. 40; this coin could also date from the very beginning of the Hellenistic period.

[18] See, however, the hypothesis of Joseph Blenkinsopp, "The Judaean Priesthood during the Neo-Babylonian and Achaemenid Periods: A Hypothetical Reconstruction," *Catholic Biblical Quar-terly* 60 (1998), pp. 25-43.

[19] See, for example, P.R. Ackroyd, *Exile and Restoration* (London, 1968), p. 34; I. Eph'al, "The Western Minorities in Babylonia in the 6th-5th Centuries B.C.: Maintenance and Cohesion," *Orientalia* 47 (1978), pp. 74-90; H.G.M. Williamson, *Ezra, Nehemiah*, World Biblical Commen-tary 16 (Waco, TX: 1985), p. 117; and Blenkinsopp, "The Social Roles of Prophets in Early Achaemenid Judah," *Journal for the Study of the Old Testament* 93 (2001), pp. 39-58.

[20] Cf. A. Ruwe, "Die Veränderung Tempel theologischer Konzepte in Ezechiel 8-11," in *Gemeinde ohne Tempel—Community without Temple. Zur Substituierung und Transformation des Jerusalemer Tempels und seines Kultes im Alten Testament, antiken Judentum und frühen Christentum*, ed. B. Ego et al., Wissenschaftliche Untersuchungen zum Neuen Testament (WUNT) 118 (Tübingen, 1999), pp. 3-18.

[21] Cf. J. Frey, "Temple and Rival Temple—The Cases of Elephantine, Mt. Gerizim, and Leontopo-lis," in *Gemeinde ohne Tempel*, ed. Ego et al., pp. 171-203; and Y. Magen, "Mt Gerizim—A Tem-ple City," *Qadmoniot* 33/2 (2000), pp. 74-118 (Hebrew).

[22] See Lemaire, "Les religions du sud de la Palestine au IVe siècle av. J.-C. d'après les ostraca araméens d'Idumée," in *Comptes rendus de l'Académie des Inscriptions et Belles Lettres* (2001), pp. 1141-1158; *Nouvelles inscriptions araméennes d'Idumée II, Collections, Moussaïeff, Jeselsohn, Welch et divers*, Suppl. n° 9 à *Transeuphratène* (Paris, 2002), pp. 149-153, 223; and "Another Temple to the Israelite God," *BAR*, September/October 2004.

[23] Cowley, *Aramaic Papyri of the Fifth Century B.C.*, nos. 30:18-19; 31:17-18 (=Grelot, *Documents araméens d'Égypte*, no. 102:17-18)

[24] Cowley, *Aramaic Papyri of the Fifth Century B.C.*, no. 32 (=Grelot, Documents araméens d'É-gypte, no.° 103).

[25] Alfred Marx, *Les offrandes végétales dans l'Ancien Testament. Du tribut d'hommage au repas escha-tologique*, SVT 57 (Leiden, 1994), pp. 145, 148.

[26] See Albani, "'Wo sollte ein Haus sein, das ihr mir bauen Könntet?' (Jes 66,1)—Schöpfung als Tempel JHWHs?" in *Gemeinde ohne Tempel*, ed. Ego et al., pp. 37-56.

[27] See A. Lange, "Gebotobservanz statt Opferkult. Zur Kultpolemik in Jer 7,1 - 8,3," in *Gemeinde ohne Tempel,* ed. Ego *et al.,* pp. 19-35.

NOTES TO CHAPTER 15

[1] See F. Hüttenmeister, *Die jüdischen Synagogen, Lehrhäuser und Gerichtshöfe,* in Hüttenmeister and G. Reeg, eds., *Die antiken Synagogen in Israel* I, BTAVO.B 12/1 (Wiesbaden, 1977); "'Synagogue" und 'Proseuchè' bei Josephus und in anderen antiken Quellen," in *Begegnungen zwischen Christentum und Judentum in Antike und Mittelalter, Festschrift H. Schreckenberg,* Schriften des Institutum Judaicum Delitzschianum 1, ed. D.A. Koch and H. Lichtenberger (Göttingen, 1993), pp. 161-181; "Die Synagogue. Ihre Entwicklung von einer multifunktionalen Einrichtung zum reinen Kultbau," in *Gemeinde ohne Tempel,* ed. Ego *et al.,* pp. 357-370; Emil Schürer, *The History of the Jewish People in the Age of Jesus Christ* (175 B.C.-A.D. 135), vol. 2, ed. G. Vermes, F. Millar and M. Black (Edinburgh, 1979), pp. 415-454; D.D. Binder, *Into the Temple Courts. The Place of the Synagogues in the Second Temple Period,* SBL.DS 169 (Atlanta, 1999); H. Bloedhorn and Hüttenmeister, "The Synagogue," in *The Cambridge History of Judaism* III, ed. W. Horbury et. al., (Cambridge, 1999), pp. 267-297; S.J.D. Cohen, "The Temple and the Synagogue," in *The Cambridge History of Judaism* III, ed. W. Horbury et al., pp. 298-325; P.W. van der Horst, "Was the Ancient Synagogue a Place of Sabbath Worship?" in *Jews, Christians and Polytheists in the Ancient Synagogue. Cultural Interaction During the Greco-Roman Period,* ed. S. Fine (London/New York, 1999), pp. 18-43; L.I. Levine, *The Ancient Synagogue. The First Thousand Years* (New Haven/London, 2000), pp. 34-73; and A. Runesson, *The Origins of the Synagogue. A Socio-Historical Study,* Coniectanca Biblica, New Testament Series (CBNTS) 37 (Stockholm, 2001); C. Claussen, *Versammlung, Gemeinde, Synagogue. Das hellenistisch-jüdische Umfeld der frühchristlichen Gemeinden,* Studien zur Umwelt des Neuen Testaments 27 (Göttingen, 2002).

[2] See J. Bright, *A History of Israel* (London, 1972), p. 439.

[3] C. Claussen, *Versammlung, Gemeinde, Synagogue,* p. 57.

[4] See W. Horbury and D. Noy, *Jewish Inscriptions of Graeco-Roman Egypt* (Cambridge, 1992), nos. 9, 27, 105; and P. Bruneau, *Recherches sur les cultes de Délos à l'époque hellénistique et à l'époque impériale* (Paris, 1970), pp. 484, 487-488.

[5] See Horbury and Noy, *Jewish Inscriptions,* no. 117.

[6] See Horbury and Noy, *Jewish Inscriptions,* no. 22.

[7] See V.A. Tcherikover and A. Fuks, eds., *Corpus Papyrorum Judaicarum* I, (Cambridge, MA: 1957-1964), pp. 239-241, no. 129.

[8] Horbury and Noy, *Jewish Inscriptions,* no. 24.

[9] Horbury and Noy, *Jewish Inscriptions,* nos. 27, 28.

[10] Horbury and Noy, *Jewish Inscriptions,* no. 25.

[11] Horbury and Noy, *Jewish Inscriptions,* nos. 9, 13.

[12] See A. Plassart, "La synagogue juive de Délos," *Revue Biblique* 11 (1914), pp. 523-534; Bruneau, *Recherches sur les cultes de Délos,* pp. 480-493; and Levine, *The Ancient Synagogue,* pp. 100-101.

[13] See H.J. Leon, *The Jews of Ancient Rome* (Philadelphia, 1960), pp. 135-166.

[14] Lemaire, "Trois inscriptions araméennes sur ossuaire et leur intérêt," *Comptes Rendus, Académie des Inscriptions & Belles-Lettres,* Janvier-Mars 2003, pp. 301-317. "Engraved in Memory," *BAR,* May/June 2006, pp. 52-57.

[15] See M.J. Martin, "Interpreting the Theodotos Inscription: Some Reflections on a First Century Jerusalem Synagogue Inscription and E.P. Sanders' 'Common Judaism'," *Ancient Near Eastern Studies* 39 (2002), pp. 160-181.

[16] The identification of this synagogue with the "synagogue of the Freedmen" in the Book of Acts

6:9 is considered as a "serious possibility" by R. Riesner ("Synagogues in Jerusalem," in *The Book of Acts in Its Palestinian Setting,* ed. R. Bauckham, The Book of Acts in its First Century Setting 4 [Grand Rapids, 1995], pp. 179-211).

[17] See Yitzhak Magen *et al.,* "Kiryat Sefer—A Jewish Village and Synagogue of the Second Temple Period," *Qadmoniot* 32/1 (1999), pp. 25-32 (Hebrew).

[18] See S. Loffreda, "Capernaum," in *The New Encypclopaedia of Archaeological Excavations in the Holy Land* I, ed. E. Stern (Jerusalem, 1993), pp. 291-295.

[19] For discussion of the identification of this synagogue, see Ehud Netzer *et al.,* "A Synagogue from the Hasmonean Period Recently Exposed in the Western Plain of Jericho," *IEJ* 49 (1999), pp. 203-221; and Y. Rapuano, "The Hasmonean Period 'Synagogue' at Jericho and the 'Council Chamber' Building at Qumran," *IEJ* 51 (2001), pp. 48-56.

[20] Acts 6:9 also mentions the presence of "Alexandrians," whose synagogue in Jerusalem is referred to in Tosephta, *Megillah* 3.6 (see J.P. Siegel, "The Alexandrians in Jerusalem and their Torah Scroll with Gold Grammata," *IEJ* 22 [1972], pp. 39-43).

[21] During the Persian period, Samaria and Idumea each had at least one temple. The Samarians built one on Mount Gerizim; and Aramaic ostraca from Idumaea refer to a "temple of YHW," probably at Khirbet el-Qom/Makkedah. Other Idumaean temples may have been located at Lachish (see O. Tufnell, *Lachish III, The Iron Age* [London, 1953], pp. 141-149; Aharoni, *Investigations at Lachish. The Sanctuary and the Residency (Lachish V)* (Tel Aviv, 1975), pp. 3-11) and Beersheba (see Herzog, "Tel Beersheba," in *The New Encyclopaedia of Archaeological Excavations in the Holy Land* I, ed. Ephraim Stern, pp. 167-173), though we do not know the deity to which these temples were dedicated. See also A. Runesson, *The Origins of the Synagogue,* CBNTS 37 (Stockholm, 2001), pp. 423-426.

[22] Thus the saying, "One has not seen a beautiful building if he has not seen the Temple" (*Sukka* 51:2); and Philo, "Of all the temples anywhere, it is the most beautiful" (*Legatio ad Caium,* 198); and the Gospel of Mark, "As he [Jesus] came out of the temple, one of his disciples said to him, 'Look, Teacher, what large stones and what large buildings!" (Mark 13:1; see also Matthew 24:1; Luke 23:5). For a discussion of this Herodian temple, see. E.-M. Laperrousaz, *Les Temples de Jérusalem* (Paris, 1999), pp. 62-84.

[23] Philo, *Legatio ad Caium,* 317-318.

[24] See J.-B. Frey, *Corpus Inscriptionum Iudaicarum* II, *Asie, Afrique* (Rome, 1952), pp. 328-330, no. 1400. For a discussion of this barrier (*soreg*) and its function, see F. Schmidt, *La pensée du Temple. De Jérusalem à Qoumrân* (Paris, 1994), pp. 95-103.

[25] Josephus, *Jewish Antiquities* 12.145.

[26] See, for example, F. Garcia Martinez and E.J.C. Tigchelaar, *The Dead Sea Scrolls. Study Edition* I (Leiden, 1997), pp. 352-353.

[27] Josephus, *Jewish War* 2.409. See also C. Mézange, "Exclusion et intégration des Romains dans l'oeuvre de Flavius Josèphe," in *Étrangers et exclus dans le monde biblique,* ed. J. Riaud, pp. 125-141.

[28] See Schürer, *The History of the Jewish People,* vol. 3 (1986), ed. Vermes *et al.,* pp. 162-169. See also F. Siegert, "Die Synagogue und das Postulat eines unblutigen Opfers," in *Gemeinde ohne Tempel,* ed. Ego *et al.,* pp. 335-356.

[29] For Delos, see Bruneau, *Recherches sur les cultes de Délos,* pp. 484, 487-488.

[30] See Schürer, *The History of the Jewish People,* vol. 3, ed. Vermes *et al.,* p. 169.

[31] See Harold W. Attridge and R.A. Oden, *Philo of Byblos. The Phoenician History,* The Catholic Biblical Quarterly Monograph Series (CBQMS) 9 (Washington, 1981), pp. 46-47, after Eusebius of Caesarea, *Preparatio Evangelica* 1.10,14-30.

[32] See, for example, George Howard, "The Tetragram and the New Testament," *Journal of Biblical Liter-*

ature 96 (1977), pp. 63-83. Note, however, that the thesis of this article remains very conjectural.

[33] For a discussion of Philo's developing an allegorical interpretation of the Temple cult while preserving the importance of the "temple built by human hands," see V. Nikiprowetzky, "La spiritualisation des sacrifices et le culte sacrificiel au temple de Jérusalem chez Philon d'Alexandrie," in Nikiprowetzky, *Études philoniennes* (Paris, 1996) (also in *Semitica* 17 [1967], pp. 97-116), pp. 79-96.

[34] Josephus's *Epitome* and the Latin version have a negative phrasing.

[35] The negative phrasing seems to correspond to the position of Philo, who describes the Essenes as "devout in the service of God, not by offering sacrifices of animals, but by resolving to sanctify their minds" (*Quod omnis probus liber sit,* 75).

[36] Josephus, *Jewish Antiquities* 18.19. See A. Baumgarten, "Josephus on Essene Sacrifice," *Journal of Jewish Studies* 45 (1994), pp. 169-183.

[37] See, for example, Caquot, "La secte de Qumrân et le Temple (Essai de synthèse)," *Revue d'Histoire et de Philolosophie Religieuse* 72 (1992), pp. 3-14; E. Puech, "Les Esséniens et le temple de Jérusalem," in *"Où demeures-tu?" (Jn 1,38). La Maison depuis le monde biblique, Mélanges Guy Couturier,* ed. J.-C. Petit (Saint-Laurent, 1994), pp. 263-286; Schmidt, *La pensée du Temple,* pp. 130-157; and Lawrence H. Schiffman, "Community Without Temple: The Qumran Community's Withdrawal from the Jerusalem Temple," in *Gemeinde ohne Tempel,* ed. Ego *et al.,* pp. 267-284: "Despite some claims to the contrary, the Sectarians did not practice sacrificial rites at Qumran. They believed, on the one hand, that sacrifice was permitted only in Jerusalem, the place that God has chosen, and on the other hand, that the rituals and priesthood of the Jerusalem Temple of their own days were illegitimate. The Sectarians saw their group as a virtual Temple."

[38] See Lemaire, "L'enseignement essénien et l'école de Qumrân," in *Hellenica et Judaica. Hommage à Valentin Nikiprowetzky,* ed. Caquot *et al.* (Leuven/Paris, 1986), pp. 191-203; "Réflexions sur la fonction du site de Qumrân," in *Josef Tadeusz Milik et le cinquantenaire de la découverte des manuscrits de la Mer Morte de Qumrân,* ed. D. Dlugosz and H. Ratajczak (Warsaw, 2000), pp. 37-43; "L'expérience essénienne de Flavius Josèphe," in *Internationales Josephus-Kolloquium Paris 2001,* ed. F. Siegert and J.U. Kalms, Münsteraner Judaistische Studien 12 (Münster, 2002), pp. 138-151.

[39] Philo, *Quod omnis probus liber sit,* 75. For a discussion of Philo's own position, see Nikiprovetzky, *Études philoniennes,* pp. 79-96.

[40] See, for example, J. Adna, "Jesus' Symbolic Act in the Temple (Mark 11:15-17): The Replacement of the Sacrificial Cult by his Atoning Death," in *Gemeinde ohne Tempel,* ed. Ego *et al.,* pp. 461-475; J. Murphy-O'Connor, "Jesus and the Money Changers (Mark 11:15-17; John 2:13-17)," *Revue Biblique* 107 (2000), pp. 42-55.

[41] This position seems typical of the thought of the "Hellenists" and close to Alexandrian allegorical exegesis (see V. Nikiprowetzky, *Études philoniennes,* (Paris, 1996) pp. 95-96).

[42] See Keel, "Warum im Jerusalemer Tempel kein anthropomorphes Kultbild gestanden haben dürfte," in *Homo Pictor,* Colloquium Rauricum 7, ed. G. Boehm (München, 2001), pp. 244-281.

[43] Tacitus, *Histories* 5.4.

[44] Josephus, *Jewish War* 5.219.

[45] Quoted in Diodorus Siculus 60.3.4; see M. Stern, *Greek and Latin Authors on Jews and Judaism* I. *From Herodotus to Plutarch* (Jerusalem, 1974), pp. 26, 28.

[46] See K. Berthelot, "Poseidonios d'Apamée et les Juifs," *Journal for the Study of Judaism* 34 (2003), pp. 160-198.

[47] Strabo 16.2.35; see Stern, *Greek and Latin Authors* I, pp. 294-300

[48] Tacitus, *Histories* 5.5.

[49] See 1 Maccabees 7:,37; Matthew 21:13; Mark 11:17; Luke 19:46. For a discussion of the

phrase, see Runesson, *The Origins of the Synagogue*, p. 429. The phrase, with a universalist emphasis, goes back to Deutero-Isaiah: "For my house shall be called a house of prayer for all peoples" (Isaiah 56:7).

NOTES TO CHAPTER 16

[1] See, for example, M. Görg, "Jahwe," in *Neues Bibel-Lexikon* 7, ed. M. Görg and B. Lang (Zürich, 1992), cols. 260-266.

[2] Compare the phrase HY LYHH in ostracon Clermont-Ganneau 152 and in seven other ostraca from the same collection. See A. Dupont-Sommer, "L'ostracon araméen du Sabbat," *Semitica* 2 (1949), pp. 29-39; "Sabbat et parascève à Éléphantine d'après des ostraca araméens inédits," in *Mémoires de l'Académie des Inscriptions et Belles Lettres* XV (1949/1950), pp. 67-88 (=Grelot, *Documents araméens d'Égypte*, no. 91; and Porten and Yardeni, *Textbook of Aramaic Documents from Ancient Egypt* IV [Jerusalem, 1999], pp. 168-169).

[3] See, for example, Eissfeldt, "Jahwe-Name und Zauberwesen. Ein Beitrag zur Frage "Religion und Magie," in *Kleine Schriften* I (Tübingen, 1962), pp. 150-171.

[4] See, for example, M. Philonenko, "L'anguipède alectorocéphale et le dieu Iaô," *Comptes rendus des séances de l'Académie des inscriptions et belles-lettres [Paris]* (1979), pp. 297-303; "Une intaille magique au nom de IAO," *Semitica* 30 (1980), pp. 57-60.

[5] See Garcia Martinez et al., *Qumran Cave 11, II, 11Q2-18, 11Q2031*, Discoveries in the Judean Desert (DJD) 23 (Oxford, 1998), pp. 181-205, pl. XXII-XXV, LIII.

[6] The origins of this phenomenon, which probably developed over a period of time, are difficult to date with precision. M. Rösel dates the earliest use of "Adonai" to the mid-third century B.C.E. because of the use of the Septuagint (*Adonaj—Warum Gott "Herr" gennant wird*, Forschungen zum Alten Testament (FAT) [Tübingen, 2000], p. 6), but the phenomenon could have started a little later since the earliest Septuagint manuscripts may have used the transcription "IAÔ."

[7] This interprétation was proposed by Nikiprowetzky: "Il semble que l'habitude de ne pas nommer Dieu procède du judaïsme hellénistique" (*De Decalogo*, Les oeuvres de Philon d'Alexandrie 23 [Paris, 1965], p. 146).

[8] See P.W. Skehan et al., *Qumran Cave 4, IV, Palaeo-Hebrew and Greek Biblical Manuscripts*, DJD 9 (Oxford, 1992), p. 168.

[9] See F. Dunand, *Papyrus grecs bibliques (Papyrus F. Inv. 266). Volumina de la Genèse et du Deutéronome* (Cairo, 1966), pp. 39-50, pl. IX-X; Z. Aly, *Three Rolls of the Early Septuagint: Genesis and Deuteronomy* (Bonn, 1980), pp. 1, 5, pl. 44-45.

[10] See W.G. Waddell, "The Tetragrammaton in the LXX," *Journal of Theological Studies* 44 (1944), pp. 157-161; Delcor, "Des diverses manières d'écrire le tétragramme sacré dans les anciens documents hébraïques," *Revue d'Histoire des Religions* 74/147 (1955), pp. 145-173; Skehan, "The Divine Name at Qumran, in the Masada Scrolls and in the Septuagint," *Bulletin of the International Organization for Septuagint and Cognate Studies* 13 (1980), pp. 14-44. This practice was known from Saint Jerome's letter (25) to Marcella: "Ninth (name): the tetragrammaton that they thought ... unutterable; it is written with the lettres *yod, he, vau* and *he*—which some people did not understand and read as *PIPI*" (see, for example, J. Labourt, *Saint Jérôme Lettres* II, Collection des Universités de France (Paris, 1951), p. 14).

[11] See E. Tov, *The Greek Minor Prophets Scroll From Nahal Hever (8 hevXIIgr)*, DJD 8 (Oxford, 1990), p. 12.

[12] See, for example, E. MacLaurin, "YHWH, the Origin of the Tetragrammaton," *Vetus Testamentum* 12 (1962), pp. 439-463.

[13] See, for example, Rösel, "Names of God," in *Encyclopedia of the Dead Sea Scrolls,* ed. Schiffman and J.C. Vanderkam (Oxford, 2000), pp. 600-602; and *Adonaj—Warum Gott "Herr" gennant wird,* pp. 207-211.

[14] Outside of Qumran other scribal techniques could be used; see J.P. Siegel, "The Alexandrians in Jerusalem and their Torah Scroll with Gold Tetragrammata," *IEJ* 22 (1972), pp. 39-43.

[15] See, for example, Eileen M. Schuller, *Non-Canonical Psalms from Qumran. A Pseudepigraphic Collection* (Atlanta, 1986), pp. 38-41.

[16] See Emanuel Tov, "Further Evidence for the Existence of a Qumran Scribal School," in *The Dead Sea Scrolls: Fifty Years after their Discovery. Proceedings of the Jerusalem Congress, July 20-25, 1997,* ed. Schiffman *et al.* (Jerusalem, 2000), pp. 199-216.

[17] 4Q176, 4Q196, 4Q382, 4Q391, 4Q443, 4Q462, 4Q524.

[18] 1QSVIII:14; 4Q531:3(=1 Samuel 25:31) and III:7 (=2 Samuel 15:8); 4Q175I:19.

[19] See, for example, E. Puech, *Qumrân Grotte 4, XVIII. Textes hébreux (4Q521-4Q528, 4Q576-4Q579),* DJD 25 (Oxford, 1998), p. 89 (4Q524).

[20] E. Tigchelaar, "In Search of the Scribe of 1QS," in *Emanuel. Studies in Hebrew Bible, Septuagint and Dead Sea Scrolls in Honor of Emanuel Tov,* ed. S.M. Paul *et al.,* SVT 94 (Leiden, 2003), pp. 439-452.

[21] See, for example, D. Barthélemy and J.T. Milik, *Qumran Cave 1,* DJD 1 (Oxford, 1955), p. 60 (1 QDtnb ad Dt 32:27); and Rösel, *Adonaj—Warum Gott "Herr" gennant wird,* pp. 211-212.

[22] See Hartmut Stegemann, "Religionsgeschichtliche Erwägungen zu den Gottesbezeichnungen in den Qumrantexten," in *Qumrân. Sa piété, sa théologie et son milieu,* ed. Delcor, BETL 46 (Paris/Leuven, 1978), pp. 195-217.

[23] See Attridge *et al., Qumran Cave 4, VIII, Parabiblical Texts,* Part 1, DJD 13 (Oxford, 1994), p. 221, pl. XV, frg. 14,3.

[24] Attridge *et al., Qumran Cave 4, VIII, Parabiblical Texts,* pp. 196, 201-202, 214-216. In the Genesis Apocryphon there appear alternating Hebrew ('LYWN) and Aramaic ('LY') forms.

[25] See Magen Broshi and Esther Eshel, "248. 4QHistorical text A (pl. IX)," in *Qumran Cave 4, XXVI. Cryptic Texts,* ed. Stephen J. Pfann *et al.,* DJD 36 (Oxford, 2000), pp. 192-200.

[26] See Garcia Martinez *et al., Qumran Cave 11,* p. 415, pl. XLVIII.

[27] See A. Wolters, "The Tetragrammaton in the Psalms Scroll," *Textus* 18 (1995), pp. 87-99. For more on this practice, which seems to have been common, see Dunand, *Papyrus grecs bibliques,* p. 13; J.P. Siegel, "The Employment of Palaeo-Hebrew Characters for the Divine Names at Qumran in the Light of Tannaitic Sources," *Hebrew Union College Annual* 42 (1971), pp. 158-171.

[28] See M. Baillet, *Qumrân Grotte 4, III (4Q482-4Q520),* DJD 7 (Oxford, 1982), pp. 226-227.

[29] See Stegemann, "Religionsgeschichtliche Erwägungen," in *Qumrân: Sa piété, sa théologie et son milieu,* ed. Delcor, pp. 195-217; Skehan, "The Divine Name at Qumran, in the Masada Scroll, and in the Septuagint," *Bulletin of the International Organization for Septuagint and Cognate Studies* 13 (1980), pp. 14-44.

[30] In the *Book of Jubilees* 23:21, the uttering of the great Name is a sign of the Apocalypse.

[31] P. Harlé and D. Pralon, *La Bible d'Alexandrie. 3. Le Lévitique* (Paris, 1988), pp. 195-196; and R. Goldenberg, "The Septuagint Ban on Cursing the Gods," *Journal for the Study of Judaism* 28 (1997), pp. 381-389.

[32] See also the comments of Philo (*On the Life of Moses* 2.114) on the vestment of the High Priest: "A piece of gold plate, too, was wrought into the form of a crown with four incisions, showing a name which only those whose ears and tongues are purified may hear or speak in the holy place, and no other person, nor in any other place at all."

[33] It is uncertain whether this refers to the celebration of Yom Kippur or the daily offering; see F.O. Fearghail, "Sir 50:5-21: Yom Kippur or the Daily Whole Offering," *Biblica* 59 (1978), pp. 301-316.

[34] We set aside here the problem of the pronunciation of the tetragammaton in the Jewish temple of Leontopolis, Egypt, built about the middle of the second century B.C.E. and destroyed by the Romans after the fall of Masada in 73 or 74 C.E.—though the use of the tetragrammaton in the Diaspora does not seem likely. On this temple, see Josephus, *Jewish War* 7.426-436 (compare 1.33); *Jewish Antiquities* 13.62-63 (compare 12.237-237, 387-388; 20.236); Mishnah *Menahot* 13(14?).10; *Tosephtah Menahot* 13.12-15; *Yeroushalmi Yoma* 6.3; *Babli Menahot* 109b; *Avodah Zarah* 52b; *Megillah* 10a; Delcor, "Le temple d'Onias en Égypte," *Revue Biblique* 75 (1968), pp. 188-205; Schürer, *The History of the Jewish People,* vol. III, ed. Geza Vermes *et al.,* pp. 47-49.

[35] See Hanan Eshel, "Josephus' View on Judaism without the Temple in Light of the Discoveries at Masada and Murabba'at," in *Gemeinde ohne Tempel,* ed. Ego *et al.,* pp. 229-238.

[36] Josephus, *Jewish Antiquities* 2.276.

[37] See J.-B. Fischer, "The Term DESPOTES in Josephus," *Jewish Quarterly Review* 49 (1958-1959), pp. 132-138.

[38] N. Walker, "The Writing of the Divine Name in Aquila and the Ben Asher Text," *Vetus Testamentum* 3 (1953), pp. 103-104; P. Katz, "YHWH = JeJÂ, YHWH = JÂJÂ?" *Vetus Testamentum* 4 (1954), pp. 428-429; and Katz, "Zur Aussprache von YHWH," *Theologische Zeitschrift* 4 (1948), pp. 467-469.

[39] This is emphasized by Rösel; see *Adonaj—Warum Gott "Herr" genannt wird,* p. 5.

[40] See, for example, F. Stolz, "Wesen und Funktion von Monotheismus," *Evangelische Theologie* 61 (2001), pp. 172-189: "Wenn es nur eine Gott gibt, braucht er keinen Eigennamen: dies ist für Judentum, Christentum and Islam selbstverständlich."

NOTES TO APPENDIX

[1] On this pronunciation and its antiquity, see B. Alfrink, "La prononciation 'Jehova' du tétragramme," *Oudtestamentische Studien* 5 (1948), pp. 43-62.

[2] See, for example, Caquot, "Le nom du Dieu d'Israël," *Positions luthériennes* 14, pp. 244-257.

[3] Diodorus Siculus, *Historical Library* I,94,2.

[4] Jerome, *Commentarium in Psalmos* 8.2: "Prius nomen domini apud Hebraeos quatuor litterarum est: *jod, he, vau, he* quod proprie Dei vocabulum sonat et legi potest IAHO, et Hebraei *arrèton,* id est, ineffabile opinantur."

[5] It is still supported by G.J. Thierry, "The Pronunciation of the Tetragrammaton," *Old Testament Studies* 5 (1948), pp. 30-42.

[6] Clement of Alexandria, *Stromates* 5.6.34.

[7] Epiphanius, *Heresies* 1.3.20; 1.3.40.5.

[8] Theodoret of Cyrrhus, *Quaestiones. XV in Exodum,* ad Ex 3.14.

[9] J. Tropper, "Der Gottesname *Yahwa,*" *Vetus Testamentum* 51 (2001), pp. 81-106.

[10] Tropper, "Der Gottesname *Yahwa,*" p. 84.

[11] See A. Lukyn Williams, "The Tetragrammaton—Jahweh, Name or Surrogate?" *Zeitschrift für die alttestamentliche Wissenschaft* 54 (1936), pp. 262-269; W. Vischer, "Eher Jahwo als Jahwe," *Theologische Zeitschrift* 16 (1960), pp. 259-267; and A. Caquot, *Positions luthériennes* 14, p. 249.

200.9 LeMaire, Andre'
LEM   The Birth of Monotheism
        The Rise and Disappearance
        Of Yahwism

DATE DUE
